Media bias

DATE DUE

NOV 0 8 2011			

Demco, Inc. 38-293

At Issue

Media Bias

Other Books in the At Issue Series:

At Issue

Media Bias

Susan Hunnicut, Book Editor

GREENHAVEN PRESS
A part of Gale, Cengage Learning

GALE
CENGAGE Learning·

Detroit • New York • San Francisco • New Haven, Conn • Waterville, Maine • London

Christine Nasso, *Publisher*
Elizabeth Des Chenes, *Managing Editor*

© 2011 Greenhaven Press, a part of Gale, Cengage Learning.

Gale and Greenhaven Press are registered trademarks used herein under license.

For more information, contact:
Greenhaven Press
27500 Drake Rd.
Farmington Hills, MI 48331-3535
Or you can visit our Internet site at gale.cengage.com

For product information and technology assistance, contact us at

Gale Customer Support, 1-800-877-4253
For permission to use material from this text or product, submit all requests online at
www.cengage.com/permissions

Further permissions questions can be emailed to permissionrequest@cengage.com

Articles in Greenhaven Press anthologies are often edited for length to meet page requirements. In addition, original titles of these works are changed to clearly present the main thesis and to explicitly indicate the author's opinion. Every effort is made to ensure that Greenhaven Press accurately reflects the original intent of the authors. Every effort has been made to trace the owners of copyrighted material.

Cover photograph reproduced by permission of Brand X Pictures.

LIBRARY OF CONGRESS CATALOGING-IN-PUBLICATION DATA

Media bias / Susan Hunnicutt, book editor.
p. cm. -- (At issue)
Includes bibliographical references and index.
ISBN 978-0-7377-5159-8 (hardcover) -- ISBN 978-0-7377-5160-4 (pbk.)
1. Mass media--Objectivity--United States. 2. Journalism--Objectivity--United States. I. Hunnicutt, Susan. II. Title. III. Series.
P96.O242U654 2011
302.23--dc22
2011001263

Printed in the United States of America
1 2 3 4 5 6 7 15 14 13 12 11

Contents

Introduction

In November 2010 American broadcast journalist Ted Koppel wrote an opinion piece for the *Washington Post* entitled "Olbermann, O'Reilly and the Death of Real News." In it he criticized cable news outlets, in particular MSNBC and Fox News, for abandoning the mission of collecting and disseminating "substantive and unbiased news." Koppel, who served for 25 years as host of ABC's *Nightline* news program, was writing in response to MSNBC's brief suspension of Keith Olbermann, host of *Countdown with Keith Olbermann*, for making unauthorized donations to three Democratic political candidates. In suspending Olbermann, MSNBC explained that the donations violated their news policy, and jeopardized Olbermann's standing as an impartial journalist. Koppel suggested that MSNBC's dismissal of Olbermann was disingenuous because it created a misleading picture of MSNBC's true journalistic values. "When Olbermann draws more than 1 million like-minded viewers to his program every night precisely because he is avowedly, unabashedly and monotonously partisan, it is not clear what misdemeanor his donations constituted," Koppel stated. "Consistency?"

The questions Koppel raised are part of an ongoing conversation about the role of journalism in society and about the professional values of journalists. The conversation is taking place in an electronic media environment that has undergone enormous changes in recent years, including the growth of cable news outlets and the movement of all news organizations into the online environment.

Koppel believes that MSNBC, Fox News, and others have abandoned key journalistic values of the past. News anchors like Walter Cronkite, Chet Huntley, David Brinkley, Frank Reynolds, and Howard K. Smith once provided "relatively unbiased accounts of information that their respective news organizations believed the public needed to know," Koppel stated in his *Washington Post* piece. They delivered the news in a way that promoted "shared perceptions and even the possibility of compromise among those who disagreed." According to Koppel, the networks supported this kind of programming, even at a financial loss, out of a belief that they were obligated to work in the public interest.

Today, however, networks and cable news providers require their news divisions to be profitable, and according to Koppel it is the relentless quest for profits that has fueled the drive toward partisanship, supported the rise of hyper-opinionated news personalities, and encouraged the embrace of their biased approach to news gathering. In pursuing this path, Koppel believes they have violated a public trust. "The need for clear, objective reporting in a world of rising religious fundamentalism, economic interdependence and global ecological problems is probably greater than it has ever been," he says. "But we are no longer a national audience receiving news from a handful of trusted gatekeepers; we're now a million or more clusters of consumers . . ." In the fragmented digital news market consumers occupy multiple, highly differentiated niches. They "harvest . . . information from like-minded providers" who tell them what they want to hear.

Koppel's comments elicited a spirited response from Keith Olbermann, who devoted a lengthy "Special Comment" on his November 15, 2010 show to respond to issues raised by Koppel. Much of Olbermann's comment focused on Walter Cronkite and another early television journalist, Edward R. Murrow. Olbermann noted that when Walter Cronkite died in 2009, he was widely praised for his objectivity and his impartiality. Paradoxically, however, the segments that were selected by multiple news outlets to illustrate Cronkite's greatness were actually moments when he made passionate and informed judgments about major news stories and then argued in their defense. Olbermann cited a fourteen-minute report on the

Watergate affair, a break-in at the Democratic National Party headquarters that "devastated the Nixon Administration" and a show on the Vietnam War in which Cronkite argued passionately that stalemate was the best result that could be hoped for, and that the United States should find an honorable way to exit the conflict.

The conclusion Olbermann drew from Cronkite's obituaries was that "deserved and heartfelt sadness at the loss of a great journalist and a great man had been turned into a metaphor for the loss of a style of utterly uninvolved, neutral, quote 'objective' reporting yet most of the highlights of the man's career had been of those moments when he correctly and fearlessly threw off those shackles and said what was true, and not merely what was factual."

Olbermann drew a similar conclusion about the work of Edward R. Murrow, whose reporting of the London Blitz of 1940 during World War II was instrumental in building support for the US entry into the war, and whose later reports at length on the career of US Senator Joseph McCarthy, called attention to a particularly dark period in the history of US politics.

"These were not glorified stenographers," Olbermann said. "These were not neutral men. These were men who did in their day what the best of journalists still try to do in this one. Evaluate, analyze, unscramble, assess—put together a coherent picture, or a challenging question—using only the facts as they can best be discerned, plus their own honesty and conscience."

James Poniewozik, blogging for *Time* a day later, concurred with Olbermann's analysis: "What journalists . . . generally call 'objectivity' is not *actual* objectivity, but something more like 'neutrality' . . . Objectivity does not mean having no opinion, taking no side or expressing no point of view. It means seeking, acknowledging and interpreting objective evidence, even when it conflicts with your preconceptions or with what you wish to be true. You can have subjective beliefs—because we all do—and yet subordinate them to objective evidence." According to Poniewozik, journalists often find themselves "distorting truth in the interests of balance." This is a significant problem which Poniewozik believes Olbermann and others are seeking to correct.

Is objectivity an essential characteristic of good journalism, or does the attempt to achieve "balance" sometimes result in the distortion of truth? Is it better for journalists to be transparent about their biases than to conceal them? Is television news today really more biased and less objective than it was in the past? These are some of the questions that are explored in *At Issue: Media Bias.*

1

How the Digital Terrain Is Changing the Way Americans Get Their News

Kristen Purcell, Lee Rainie, Amy Mitchell, Tom Rosenstiel, and Kenny Olmstead

Kristen Purcell, Lee Rainie, Amy Mitchell, Tom Rosenstiel, and Kenny Olmstead are on staff at the Pew Research Center, a nonpartisan, nonprofit "fact tank" that provides information on the issues, attitudes, and trends shaping America and the world. The Pew Research Center's Project for Excellence in Journalism is dedicated to trying to understand the information revolution.

American's access to news coverage has changed in significant ways as a result of the Internet. Social networking sites that allow individuals to post stories in public places and comment on them have changed the news, making it a more social experience. The news cycle has also become more pervasive in life, as many people have adopted smart phones that make the news portable. In spite of having many news outlets to choose from, individuals tend to rely on a limited number of news sources. Almost two-thirds of those surveyed report that major news organizations do a good job of covering stories that are important to them. Republicans are more likely than Democrats to say that news coverage is biased.

In the digital era, news has become omnipresent. Americans access it in multiple formats on multiple platforms on myriad devices. The days of loyalty to a particular news organization on a particular piece of technology in a particular form are gone. The overwhelming majority of Americans (92%) use multiple platforms to get news on a typical day, including national TV, local TV, the internet, local newspapers, radio, and national newspapers. *Some 46% of Americans say they get news from four to six media platforms on a typical day. Just 7% get their news from a single media platform on a typical day.*

The internet is at the center of the story of how people's relationship to news is changing. Six in ten Americans (59%) get news from a combination of online *and* offline sources on a typical day, and the internet is now the third most popular news platform, behind local television news and national television news.

The advent of social media like social networking sites and blogs has helped the news become a social experience in fresh ways for consumers.

Foraging and Opportunism

The process Americans use to get news is based on foraging and opportunism. They seem to access news when the spirit moves them or they have a chance to check up on headlines. At the same time, gathering the news is not entirely an open-ended exploration for consumers, even online where there are limitless possibilities for exploring news. While online, most people say they use between two and five online news sources and 65% say they do not have a single favorite website for news. Some 21% say they routinely rely on just one site for their news and information.

In this new multi-platform media environment, people's relationship to news is becoming portable, personalized, and participatory. These new metrics stand out:

- *Portable*: 33% of cell phone owners now access news on their cell phones.

- *Personalized*: 28% of internet users have customized their home page to include news from sources and on topics that particularly interest them.

- *Participatory*: 37% of internet users have contributed to the creation of news, commented about it, or disseminated it via postings on social media sites like Facebook or Twitter.

To a great extent, people's experience of news, especially on the internet, is becoming a shared social experience as people swap links in emails, post news stories on their social networking site feeds, highlight news stories in their Tweets, and haggle over the meaning of events in discussion threads. For instance, more than 8 in 10 online news consumers get or share links in emails.

Two Trends

The rise of the internet as a news platform has been an integral part of these changes. This report discusses two significant technological trends that have influenced news consumption behavior: First, the advent of social media like social networking sites and blogs has helped the news become a social experience in fresh ways for consumers. People use their social networks *and* social networking technology to filter, assess, and react to news. Second, the ascent of mobile connectivity via smart phones has turned news gathering and news awareness into an anytime, anywhere affair for a segment of avid news watchers.

These are some of the key findings to come out of a new survey by the Pew Internet & American Life Project and the

Project for Excellence in Journalism aimed at understanding the new news landscape. Below are some of the other key findings:

The internet has surpassed newspapers and radio in popularity as a news platform on a typical day and now ranks just behind TV.

More than half of American adults (56%) say they follow the news "all or most of the time," and another quarter (25%) follow the news at least "some of the time." Asked specifically about their news habits on "a typical day," the results are striking: 99% of American adults say that on a typical day, they get news from at least one of these media platforms: a local or national print newspaper, a local or national television news broadcast, radio, or the internet.[1]

The majority of online news consumers (57%) say they routinely rely on just two to five websites for their news.

Only local and national TV news, the latter if you combine cable and network, are more popular platforms than the

---

1. Note that our question framing in the current survey is somewhat different from surveys that ask about consumers' news consumption behavior "yesterday" or about the specific frequency of their news consumption. Instead, in the current survey, respondents were asked in one question whether, on a typical day, they get news from each of the following: local television news; national television news; local print newspapers; national print newspapers; or radio. Later in the survey, those who were identified as being at least occasional online news consumers were asked if, on a typical day, they get news from any one of 14 different online sources, ranging from the website of a national newspaper or television news organization to Facebook or Twitter posts of journalists, news organizations, or other people they follow. When answers to the two questions are combined, 99% of American adults say that on a typical day, they use at least one of the 5 traditional news sources or 14 online news sources asked about. This number may be higher than other estimates of daily news consumption because 1) respondents are asked about a "typical day" rather than "yesterday," and 2) they are asked about a number of "non-traditional" news sources which may prompt them to recall behavior they might not otherwise consider when asked about their daily news consumption.

internet for news. And most Americans use a combination of both online and offline sources. On a typical day:

- 78% of Americans say they get news from a local TV station

- 73% say they get news from a national network such as CBS or cable TV station such as CNN or FoxNews

- 61% say they get some kind of news online

- 54% say they listen to a radio news program at home or in the car

- 50% say they read news in a local newspaper

- 17% say they read news in a national newspaper such as the *New York Times* or *USA Today*.

Many Platforms

Americans today routinely get their news from multiple sources and a mix of platforms. Nine in ten American adults (92%) get news from multiple platforms on a typical day, with half of those using four to six platforms daily. Fully 59% get news from a combination of online and offline sources on a typical day. Just over a third (38%) rely solely on offline sources, and 2% rely exclusively on the internet for their daily news.

The average online consumer regularly turns to only a few websites.

Most news consumers utilize multiple platforms for news, but online their range of specific outlets is limited. The majority of online news consumers (57%) say they routinely rely on just two to five websites for their news. Only 11% say they get their news from more than five websites, and 21% regularly rely on just one site.

Moreover, many do not have strong loyalty to particular online sources. When asked whether they have a favorite online news source, the majority of online news users (65%) say they do not. Among those who do, the most popular sites are those of major news organizations such as such as CNN and Fox.

Internet users use the web for a range of news, but local is not near the top of the list.

The most popular online news subjects are the weather (followed by 81% of internet news users), national events (73%), health and medicine (66%), business and the economy (64%), international events (62%), and science and technology (60%).

Asked what subjects they would like to receive more coverage, 44% said scientific news and discoveries, 41% said religion and spirituality, 39% said health and medicine, 39% said their state government, and 38% said their neighborhood or local community.

News consumption is a socially-engaging and socially-driven activity, especially online. The public is clearly part of the news process now. Participation comes more through sharing than through contributing news themselves.

Getting news is often an important social act. Some 72% of American news consumers say they follow the news because they enjoy talking with others about what is happening in the world and 69% say keeping up with the news is a social or civic obligation. And 50% of American news consumers say they rely to some degree on people around them to tell them the news they need to know. Online, the social experience is widespread:

- 75% of online news consumers say they get news forwarded through email or posts on social networking sites and 52% say they share links to news with others via those means.

- 51% of social networking site (e.g. Facebook) users who are also online news consumers say that on a typical day they get news items from people they follow. Another 23% of this cohort follow news organizations or individual journalists on social networking sites.

Content That Encourages Interaction

Some 37% of internet users have contributed to the creation of news, commentary about it, or dissemination of news via social media. They have done at least one of the following: commenting on a news story (25%); posting a link on a social networking site (17%); tagging content (11%), creating their own original news material or opinion piece (9%), or Tweeting about news (3%).

News is pocket-sized.

Some 80% of American adults have cell phones today, and 37% of them go online from their phones. The impact of this new mobile technology on news gathering is unmistakable. One quarter (26%) of all Americans say they get some form of news via cell phone today—that amounts to 33% of cell phone owners. These wireless news consumers get the following types of news on their phones: . . .

- Weather: 26

- News and current events: 25

- An application for news content: 16

- Sports scores and stories: 16

- Traffic info: 13

- Financial info: 12

- News via emails and texts: 11

Wireless news consumers have fitted this "on-the-go" access to news into their already voracious news-gathering habits. They use multiple news media platforms on a typical day, forage widely on news topics, and browse the web for a host of subjects.

News is personalized: The "Daily Me" takes shape.

Some 28% of internet users have customized their home page to include news from their favorite source or topics and 40% of internet users say an important feature of a news website to them is the ability to customize the news they get from the site. Moreover, 36% of internet users say an important part of a news website to them is the ability to manipulate content themselves such as graphics, maps, and quizzes.

Liberals and Democrats are more likely to say the big news organizations do a good job on subjects that matter to them, while conservatives and Republicans are the ones most likely to see coverage as biased.

News is easier to follow now, but overwhelming. And most topics get plenty of coverage, in Americans' eyes.

Americans send mixed messages in the survey about how they feel in a world where news is updated constantly and they can access news all the time. We asked respondents about how the volume of news might play into this: "Compared with five years ago, do you think it is easier or harder to keep up with news and information today?" Some 55% say it is easier, only 18% say it is harder. One quarter of adults (25%) say there is no difference between now and five years ago.

Yet even as they say it is easier to keep up with the news, Americans still feel overwhelmed. Fully 70% agreed with that statement: "The amount of news and information available from different sources today is overwhelming." Some 25% "completely agreed" with that statement and 45% "mostly agreed."

Good news, bad news about media performance.

When it comes to the quality of coverage itself, respondents give correspondingly mixed signals. Just under two-thirds (63%) agree with statement that "major news organizations do a good job covering all of the important news stories and subjects that matter to me." Yet 72% also back the idea that "most news sources today are biased in their coverage." Some of the explanation for this dichotomy seems to be rooted in the views of partisans. Liberals and Democrats are more likely to say the big news organizations do a good job on subjects that matter to them, while conservatives and Republicans are the ones most likely to see coverage as biased.

2

The Media Have Always Been Biased

Jeremy D. Boreing

Jeremy Boreing is a screenwriter and film producer. His work has appeared at Newsbusters.org and Breitbart.com.

It is wrong to believe that the mainstream media strive for objectivity or that they have ever attained it. American history demonstrates that the press has always been partisan and deeply involved in politics. The media have always provided a platform for specific biases. What should be more feared than bias and competition is the appearance of objectivity—faux fairness—that conceals real motivations and commitments.

By now, readers of *Big Journalism* are more than familiar with the liberal media's exercise in conspiracy, collusion, and confusion that was the JournoList. [JournoList was a private Google Group moderated by blogger and columnist Ezra Klein. In 2010 the group was deleted after a series of controversial emails were leaked, resulting in accusations of collusion between liberal and progressive politicians and the political press.]

For most on the political right, the leaked emails being exposed by Tucker Carlson and his DailyCaller website serve as proof that the Mainstream Media has jumped the shark, compromising its traditional credibility and betraying a deep, passionate left-wing bias beneath what was supposed to be objective journalism.

But while all of that is certainly true, I believe it is based on a flawed premise. Specifically, that the Mainstream Media has ever been—or even should have ever been—credible and objective.

The historic reality is that media in America has always been a tool of partisans. During the years preceding the American Revolution, the revolutionary founders used the pages of the emergent colonial newspapers to rally support for their petitions against the crown. In fact, newspapers were perhaps the most powerful tools in moving public opinion in favor of independence, both through publication of stories hostile to British intentions, or editorial tracts promoting revolution.

A Tool for Partisans

The most famous man in America at the time of the Revolution was Benjamin Franklin, [whose] own paper, the *Pennsylvania Gazette*, carried America's first political cartoon—JOIN OR DIE—penned by Franklin himself. Of course, Franklin was also a Founding Father of the nation with a seat in both the Continental Congress, and on the more exclusive subcommittee that drafted the Declaration of Independence. Certainly the *Gazette*, then, lacked objectivity, if not credibility.

When, after the war, the first Congress under the new Constitution passed the First Amendment, securing freedom of the press in the new nation, it was not a fair, unbiased press they were defending but the gritty, partisan, error (if not patently fabrication)-prone press of the Revolution.

While this sort of manipulative, partisan press may sound radical and inappropriate to modern Americans, the truth is, it has always been this way.

When the second President of the United States signed the Sedition Act, granting the federal government the power to imprison journalists who printed utter falsehoods, he may have lacked Constitutional and moral justification, but he was not without cause.

Anti-Federalist provocateurs like Benjamin Franklin Bache, grandson of the Founding Franklin, spread the most salacious stories about the fledgling American government under the Federalist party, largely to promote support (in the likely event of war with Britain) for the French Revolution. It was not only through editorializing that the Bache's *Aurora* and other newspapers pushed this agenda, but through hard—if selective—reporting on British atrocities against American interests and blatant omission of French ones. The smear campaign reached such heights that President [John] Adams actually feared for his life.

For their part, the Federalists, guided by Alexander Hamilton, also sought to sway public opinion toward war with France using the same questionable techniques.

It Has Always Been This Way

While this sort of manipulative, partisan press may sound radical and inappropriate to modern Americans, the truth is, it has always been this way.

When [Thomas] Jefferson sought the Presidency in 1800, he did not campaign. That was still considered unseemly in the political culture of the day. He did, however, pump money into Republican newspapers, not for ads, but for advocacy.

Abraham Lincoln actually shut down newspapers that he saw as hostile to Union goals or dangerous to Union strategy, and newspaper magnates of the industrial revolution drove politics in this country. They even gave their papers names like *The Democrat*. How objective could such a paper actually be?

In fact, it wasn't until the twentieth century that the idea of a transcendent press really became dominant and Americans began to accept journalism at face value. But had journalism actually changed, or were Americans, united against the common enemies of Depression, Nazism, and the Imperial Japanese simply in enough general political agreement to temporarily believe the media represented them all while it really continued to pursue its own partisan agenda?

Consider the great pillars of late twentieth century news— Walter Cronkite, Peter Jennings, Dan Rather, etc. . . . These men were the very embodiment of the ideal of seemingly objective journalism. Yet, Walter Cronkite—"the most trusted man in America"—was hardly non-partisan. He was a member of the World Federalist Association, calling for the end of American hegemony and ceding of American sovereignty to a one-world government. He was a supporter, even with CBS resources, of the anti-war movement during Vietnam. His declaration that that war was unwinnable altered history forever, swaying public opinion and even convincing President [Lyndon B.] Johnson that the jig might actually be up.

The virgin media of our youth did not exist, and it should not exist. As with every other facet of life in a free society, it is only competition that creates progress and openness.

Peter Jennings dated Palestinian activist Hanan Ashrawi while serving as ABC's Bureau Chief in Beirut and conducted the first-ever western interview with [Palestinian leader] Yasser Arafat. Was it only coincidence then that he refused to call the Black September terrorists who kidnapped and killed the Israeli athletes at the [1972] Munich Olympics terrorists?

And of course, Dan Rather lost his job over the Killian Documents scandal [2004] in which CBS published obvious forgeries of National Guard papers criticizing the military service of President George W. Bush. As if in answer to the question of credibility and objectivity, Mr. Rather defended his erroneous reporting as perhaps, "fake, but accurate."

Did none of this apparent bias affect any of the rest of the decades of news these men and their small cadre of equally liberal peers covered, or was there simply no alternative media to highlight their bias in the post-World War Two America? When seasoned media professionals fondly reminisce about the days when President [Franklin D.] Roosevelt could be in a wheelchair or President [John F.] Kennedy could openly liaise with myriad women, aren't they really harkening to a day when no one questioned their open liberal biases? Did the public not have the right to know that their President was in a wheelchair, or a philanderer? Is it up to the media if a voter chooses to factor health and moral standing and honesty in their voting decisions?

A Bullhorn for Specific Biases

For all of the talk about a fourth branch of government, calling to account corruption on both sides of the aisle, and informing the people's decisions with transcendent objectivity, the media has always been a bullhorn for specific biases. The virgin media of our youth did not exist, and it should not exist. As with every other facet of life in a free society, it is only competition that creates progress and openness. In media, this means diverse views and diverse sources, calling not only corrupt politicians into account, but each other as well.

As distasteful as openly partisan media may be, it is the media of the twentieth-century that should be most feared—where the illusion of fairness masks the great deceit of the people. It is the media of the twentieth-century that gave such rapid rise to the ideas of globalism and socialism, because that is the media that championed them unchecked and quietly but consistently for more than fifty years.

So rather than decrying the JournoList as a bad thing, I choose to celebrate it for further illuminating the true state of things. The Mainstream Media is exceedingly, socially, and politically liberal. It has been for years, and its high-time the charade was finally ended. Only the emergence of an equally biased, right-wing media exposed the list, and only that same new media can continue to break down the left-wing media's faux-fairness front to reveal them for what they really are. In the balance that might one day exist between left-media and right-media, a better quality of journalism will emerge—one where sloppy, selective, dishonest reporting is instantly revealed by the opposition. People will get better news, they just may have to work harder to get it than just flipping on CBS in the evenings and getting lied to with a straight face for an hour.

And who knows, maybe in this truly competitive environment, a market will emerge for a genuinely fair and balanced media that holds itself to a higher standard than anything we have ever seen before.

3

Journalists Must Strive for Objectivity

David Brooks

David Brooks is a columnist for the New York Times *and a regular analyst on* Newshour with Jim Lehrer. *He is the author of two books,* Bobos in Paradise: The New Upper Class and How They Got There *and* On Paradise Drive: How We Live Now (and Always Have) in the Future Tense.

Truth exists, truth can be known, and objectivity is something journalists have to aspire to. For other professions, objectivity is less important than the ability to be a team player. But for journalists, including opinion journalists, objectivity is essential. Objectivity requires a willingness to look at all the facts, to rise above the stereotypes, and to be able to see the big picture.

There is some dispute about whether objectivity can really exist. How do we know the truth? Well, I'm not a relativist on the subject. I think there is truth out there and that objectivity is like virtue; it's the thing you always fall short of, but the thing you always strive toward. And by the way, I think that opinion journalists have to be objective just as much as straight reporters. Opinion journalists, too, have to be able to see reality wholly and truly. As [British author] George Orwell said, they have to face unpleasant facts just as much as anybody else.

David Brooks, "Objectivity in Journalism," *Imprimis* 35 no. 1, January 2006. Copyright © 2006 by Brooks Newspapers. Reproduced by permission.

The Ability to Suspend Judgments

What are the stages of getting to objectivity? The first stage is what somebody called negative capacity—the ability to suspend judgment while you're looking at the facts. Sometimes when we look at a set of facts, we like to choose the facts that make us feel good because it confirms our worldview. But if you're going to be objective—and this is for journalists or anybody else—surely the first stage is the ability to look at *all* the facts, whether they make you feel good or not.

Walter Lipmann once noted that most journalism is about the confirmation of stereotypes—preexisting generalizations we all have in our heads. The ability to ignore these stereotypes is crucial to objectivity.

The second stage is modesty. And here I think one of the great models of journalism is someone we just saw at a Senate confirmation hearing—Chief Justice John Roberts. He was asked by the Senators to *emote*. Senator Dianne Feinstein, for instance, asked him how he would react as a father to a certain case. It was as if she and other Senators wanted him to weep on camera. They wanted him to do the sentimental thing, in order to make them feel that he was one of them. But he absolutely refused, because his ethos as a lawyer and as a judge is not about self-exposure. It's about self-control. It's about playing a role in society—a socially useful role. Roberts kept explaining that judges wear black robes because it's not about them; it's not about narcissism. It's about doing a job for society. Judges have to suppress some of themselves in order to read the law fairly and not prejudge cases.

The same thing has to happen for journalists. We live in an age of self-exposure. But journalists have to suppress their egos so that they can see the whole truth, whether they like it or not.

The third stage of objectivity is the ability to process data—to take all the facts that you've accumulated and honestly process them into a pattern. This is a mysterious activity called judgment. How do you take all the facts that are in front of you and fit them into one pattern? If you pick up a cup of coffee, one part of your brain senses how heavy it is. Another part of your brain senses how hot it is. Another part of your brain senses the shape of the cup. Another part of your brain knows that you're shaking, which creates ripples across the surface of the coffee. All these parts are disconnected and we have no idea how the human brain processes that information. But some people are really good at connecting the dots and seeing the patterns and other people are not. And surely that's the third stage of objectivity—the ability to take all the data, not just the data you like, and form it into a generalizable whole.

Loyalty to the Truth

The fourth stage of objectivity is the ability to betray friends. In Washington, there's loyalty to the truth and loyalty to your team. And in government, loyalty to your team is sometimes more important than loyalty to the truth. If you're a U.S. Senator, you can't tell the truth all the time. If you work for an administration, you can't tell the truth all the time, because government is a team sport. The only way you can get something done is collectively—as a group. It takes a majority to pass a piece of legislation. It takes an administration working together to promulgate a policy. And that's fine. Politicians betray the truth all the time in favor of loyalty to a higher good for them. But for journalists and for most citizens, loyalty to the truth should supplant loyalty to the team. And frankly, that no longer happens enough. For example, when I came to the *New York Times*, there was a guy at the *Times* named Paul Krugman writing against President [George W.] Bush twice a week. I had to decide whether I wanted to be the anti-

Krugman and write pro-Bush columns every week. It would have been good for the team. But I decided it wouldn't be good for the truth. So I decided not to do that.

The fifth stage of objectivity is the ability to ignore stereotypes. This is the oldest rule of journalism. [American journalist] Walter Lipmann once noted that most journalism is about the confirmation of stereotypes—preexisting generalizations we all have in our heads. The ability to ignore these stereotypes is crucial to objectivity.

And the last bit, the sixth stage, is a willingness to be a little dull. It's easy to write a lambasting, vitriolic attack on someone. But usually—unless that person is [Nazi dictator] Adolf Hitler—that's not fair.

I'm someone who fails every day at being objective. But I still think that's the old-fashioned virtue that has to be respected above the good of partisan opinion—the reason being, again, that there is something that exists out there called truth.

4

Journalism's Quest for Objectivity Has Actually Created a Moral Void

Chris Hedges

Chris Hedges has worked as a foreign correspondent for The Christian Science Monitor, National Public Radio, *the* Dallas Morning News *and the* New York Times. *He was part of the team of reporters at the* New York Times *awarded a Pulitzer Prize in 2002 for the paper's coverage of global terrorism.*

The idea that objectivity is a value and a virtue in journalism has been used by corporate interests to neutralize public opinion. Reporting grounded in a commitment to justice would raise questions and stimulate debate about structure, laws, privilege, power, and justice. Truth is multi-faceted, and issues have more than two sides. But most journalists, who like to see themselves as independent, are actually corporate employees, who exist in a symbiotic relationship with the power elite. They do not have voices of their own. The traditional press obscures real and pressing questions in order to preserve structures of power.

Reporters who witness the worst of human suffering and return to newsrooms angry see their compassion washed out or severely muted by the layers of editors who stand between the reporter and the reader. The creed of objectivity and balance, formulated at the beginning of the 19th century by newspaper owners to generate greater profits from advertisers, disarms and cripples the press.

Chris Hedges, "The Creed of Objectivity Killed the News," *Truthdig*, February 1, 2010. This column was originally published on *Truthdig* (www.truthdig.com). Copyright © 2010 by Truthdig.com. Reproduced by permission.

And the creed of objectivity becomes a convenient and profitable vehicle to avoid confronting unpleasant truths or angering a power structure on which news organizations depend for access and profits. This creed transforms reporters into neutral observers or voyeurs. It banishes empathy, passion and a quest for justice. Reporters are permitted to watch but not to feel or to speak in their own voices. They function as "professionals" and see themselves as dispassionate and disinterested social scientists. This vaunted lack of bias, enforced by bloodless hierarchies of bureaucrats, is the disease of American journalism.

Truth . . . A Slippery Little Bugger

"The very notion that on any given story all you have to do is report what both sides say and you've done a fine job of objective journalism debilitates the press," the late columnist Molly Ivins once wrote [in a 2007 *New York Times* article] "There is no such thing as objectivity, and the truth, that slippery little bugger, has the oddest habit of being way to hell off on one side or the other: it seldom nestles nearly halfway between any two opposing points of view. The smug complacency of much of the press—I have heard many an editor say, 'Well, we're being attacked by both sides so we must be right'—stems from the curious notion that if you get a quote from both sides, preferably in an official position, you've done the job. In the first place, most stories aren't two-sided, they're 17-sided at least. In the second place, it's of no help to either the readers or the truth to quote one side saying, 'Cat,' and the other side saying 'Dog,' while the truth is there's an elephant crashing around out there in the bushes."

Ivins went on to write that "the press's most serious failures are not its sins of commission, but its sins of omission—the stories we miss, the stories we don't see, the stories that don't hold press conferences, the stories that don't come from 'reliable sources.'"

This abject moral failing has left the growing numbers of Americans shunted aside by our corporate state without a voice. It has also, with the rise of a ruthless American oligarchy, left the traditional press on the wrong side of our growing class divide. The elitism, distrust and lack of credibility of the press—and here I speak of the dwindling institutions that attempt to report news—come directly from this steady and willful disintegration of the media's moral core.

As long as one viewpoint is balanced by another ... the job of a reporter is deemed complete. But this is more often a way to obscure rather than expose truth.

This moral void has been effectively exploited by the 24-hour cable news shows and trash talk radio programs. The failure of the fact-based press to express empathy or outrage for our growing underclass has permitted the disastrous rise of "faith-based" reporting. The bloodless and soulless journalism of the traditional media has bolstered the popularity of partisan outlets that present a view of the world that often has no relation to the real, but responds very effectively to the emotional needs of viewers. Fox News is, in some sense, no more objective than *The New York Times*, but there is one crucial and vital difference. Fox News and most of the other cable outlets do not feel constrained by verifiable facts. Within the traditional news establishment, facts may have been self-selected or skillfully stage-managed by public relations specialists, but what was not verifiable was not publishable.

The cable news channels have cleverly seized on the creed of objectivity and redefined it in populist terms. They attack news based on verifiable fact for its liberal bias, for, in essence, failing to be objective, and promise a return to "genuine" objectivity. Fox's Bill O'Reilly argues, "If Fox News is a conservative channel—and I'm going to use the word 'if'—so what? ... You've got 50 other media that are blatantly left. Now, I don't think Fox is a conservative channel. I think it's a traditional channel. There's a difference. We are willing to hear points of view that you'll never hear on ABC, CBS or NBC."

Does Universal Truth Have an American Accent?

O'Reilly is not wrong in suggesting that the objectivity of the traditional media has an inherent political bias. But it is a bias that caters to the power elite and it is a bias that is confined by fact. The traditional quest for "objectivity" is, as [communications theorist] James Carey wrote, also based on an ethnocentric conceit: "It pretended to discover Universal Truth, to proclaim Universal Laws, and to describe a Universal Man. Upon inspection it appeared, however, that its Universal Man resembled a type found around Cambridge, Massachusetts, or Cambridge, England; its Universal Laws resembled those felt to be useful by Congress and Parliament; and its Universal Truth bore English and American accents."

Objectivity creates the formula of quoting Establishment specialists or experts within the narrow confines of the power elite who debate policy nuance like medieval theologians. As long as one viewpoint is balanced by another, usually no more than what Sigmund Freud [the founder of psychoanalysis] would term "the narcissism of minor difference," the job of a reporter is deemed complete. But this is more often a way to obscure rather than expose truth.

Reporting, while it is presented to the public as neutral, objective and unbiased, is always highly interpretive. It is defined by rigid stylistic parameters. I have written, like most other reporters, hundreds of news stories. Reporters begin with a collection of facts, statements, positions and anecdotes and then select those that create the "balance" permitted by the formula of daily journalism. The closer reporters get to official sources, for example those covering Wall Street, Congress, the White House or the State Department, the more constraints they endure. When reporting depends heavily on access it becomes very difficult to challenge those who grant or deny that access. This craven desire for access has turned huge sections of the Washington press, along with most business reporters, into courtiers. The need to be included in press briefings and background interviews with government or business officials, as well as the desire for leaks and early access to official documents, obliterates journalistic autonomy.

Ethical questions open journalism to the nebulous world of interpretation and philosophy, and for this reason journalists flee from ethical inquiry like a herd of frightened sheep.

"Record the fury of a Palestinian whose land has been taken from him by Israeli settlers—but always refer to Israel's 'security needs' and its 'war on terror,'" Robert Fisk [Middle East Correspondent for the *The Independent*] writes. "If Americans are accused of 'torture', call it 'abuse'. If Israel assassinates a Palestinian, call it a 'targeted killing'. If Armenians lament their Holocaust of 1,500,000 souls in 1915, remind readers that Turkey denies this all too real and fully documented genocide. If Iraq has become a hell on earth for its people, recall how awful Saddam [Hussein] was. If a dictator is on our side, call him a 'strongman', If he's our enemy, call him a tyrant, or part of the 'axis of evil'. And above all else, use the word 'terrorist.' Terror, terror, terror, terror, terror, terror, terror. Seven days a week."

"Ask 'how' and 'who'—but not 'why,'" Fisk adds. "Source everything to officials: 'American officials', 'intelligence officials', 'official sources', anonymous policemen or army officers. And if these institutions charged with our protection abuse their power, then remind readers and listeners and viewers of the dangerous age in which we now live, the age of terror—which means that we must live in the Age of the Warrior, someone whose business and profession and vocation and mere existence is to destroy our enemies."

Real Objectivity Requires Hard Work and Tolerance

"In the classic example, a refugee from Nazi Germany who appears on television saying monstrous things are happening in his homeland must be followed by a Nazi spokesman saying Adolf Hitler is the greatest boon to humanity since pasteurized milk," the former *New York Times* columnist Russell Baker wrote. "Real objectivity would require not only hard work by news people to determine which report was accurate, but also a willingness to put up with the abuse certain to follow publication of an objectively formed judgment. To escape the hard work or the abuse, if one man says Hitler is an ogre, we instantly give you another to say Hitler is a prince. A man says the rockets won't work? We give you another who says they will. The public may not learn much about these fairly sensitive matters, but neither does it get another excuse to denounce the media for unfairness and lack of objectivity. In brief, society is teeming with people who become furious if told what the score is."

Journalists, because of their training and distaste for shattering their own exalted notion of themselves, lack the inclination and vocabulary to discuss ethics. They will, when pressed, mumble something about telling the truth and serving the public. They prefer not to face the fact that my truth is not your truth. News is a signal, a "blip," an alarm that something is happening beyond our small circle of existence, as Walter Lippmann noted in his book *Public Opinion*. Journalism does not point us toward truth since, as Lippmann understood, there is always a vast divide between truth and news. Ethical questions open journalism to the nebulous world of interpretation and philosophy, and for this reason journalists flee from ethical inquiry like a herd of frightened sheep.

Journalists Are Corporate Employees

Journalists, while they like to promote the image of themselves as fierce individualists, are in the end another species of
corporate employees. They claim as their clients an amor-
phous public. They seek their moral justification in the service
of this nameless, faceless mass and speak little about the vast
influence of the power elite to shape and determine reporting.
Does a public even exist in a society as fragmented and di-
vided as ours? Or is the public, as Walter Lippmann wrote,
now so deeply uninformed and divorced from the inner work-
ings of power and diplomacy as to make it a clean slate on
which our armies of skilled propagandists can, often through
the press, leave a message?

---

*Real reporting, grounded in a commitment to justice and
empathy, could have informed and empowered the public
as we underwent a corporate coup d'etat in slow motion.*

The symbiotic relationship between the press and the
power elite worked for nearly a century. It worked as long as
our power elite, no matter how ruthless or insensitive, was
competent. But once our power elite became incompetent and
morally bankrupt, the press, along with the power elite, lost
its final vestige of credibility. The press became, as seen in the
Iraq war and the aftermath of the financial upheavals, a class
of courtiers. The press, which has always written and spoken
from presuppositions and principles that reflect the elite consensus, now peddles a consensus that is flagrantly artificial.
Our elite oversaw the dismantling of the country's manufac-
turing base and the betrayal of the working class with the pas-
sage of the North American Free Trade Agreement and the
press dutifully trumpeted this as a form of growth. Our elite
deregulated the banking industry, leading to nationwide bank
collapses, and the press extolled the value of the free market.

Our elite corrupted the levers of power to advance the interests of corporations and the press naively conflated freedom with the free market. This reporting may have been "objective" and "impartial" but it defied common sense. The harsh reality of shuttered former steel-producing towns and growing human misery should have, in the hands of any good cop reporter, exposed the fantasies. But the press long ago stopped thinking and lost nearly all its moral autonomy.

Justice, Empathy, and Real Debate

Real reporting, grounded in a commitment to justice and empathy, could have informed and empowered the public as we underwent a corporate coup d'etat in slow motion. It could have stimulated a radical debate about structures, laws, privilege, power and justice. But the traditional press, by clinging to an outdated etiquette designed to serve corrupt power structures, lost its social function. Corporations, which once made many of these news outlets very rich, have turned to more effective forms of advertising. Profits have plummeted. And yet these press courtiers, lost in the fantasy of their own righteousness and moral probity, cling to the hollow morality of "objectivity" with comic ferocity.

The world will not be a better place when these fact-based news organizations die. We will be propelled into a culture where facts and opinions will be interchangeable, where lies will become true, and where fantasy will be peddled as news. I will lament the loss of traditional news. It will unmoor us from reality. The tragedy is that the moral void of the news business contributed as much to its own annihilation as the protofascists who feed on its carcass.

5

It Is Naïve to Think That Journalists Can Avoid Bias

Andrew R. Cline

Andrew R. Cline is an associate professor of journalism at Missouri State University.

Bias is a characteristic of all communication. To identify bias in a message is to understand its historical, social, political context, and the nature of its influences. The presence of bias does not imply that a message is untruthful. Claims of bias in the media are often delivered as complaints, implying that the press as a whole unfairly favors one side or the other. This is an oversimplification that fails to explain the rich diversity of influences that impact the environment in which news reporting occurs.

There is no such thing as an objective point of view.

No matter how much we may try to ignore it, human communication always takes place in a context, through a medium, and among individuals and groups who are situated historically, politically, economically, and socially. This state of affairs is neither bad nor good. It simply is. Bias is a small word that identifies the collective influences of the entire context of a message.

Politicians are certainly biased and overtly so. They belong to parties and espouse policies and ideologies. And while they may think their individual ideologies are simply common sense, they understand that they speak from political positions.

Journalists, too, speak from political positions but usually not overtly so. The journalistic ethics of objectivity and fairness are strong influences on the profession. But journalistic objectivity is not the pristine objectivity of philosophy. Instead, a journalist attempts to be objective by two methods: 1) fairness to those concerned with the news and 2) a professional process of information gathering that seeks fairness, completeness, and accuracy. As we all know, the ethical heights journalists set for themselves are not always reached. But, all in all, like politics, it is an honorable profession practiced, for the most part, by people trying to do the right thing.

The press is often thought of as a unified voice with a distinct bias (right or left depending on the critic). This simplistic thinking fits the needs of ideological struggle, but is hardly useful in coming to a better understanding of what is happening in the world. I believe journalism is an under-theorized practice. In other words, journalists often do what they do without reflecting upon the meaning of the premises and assumptions that support their practice. I say this as a former journalist. I think we may begin to reflect upon journalistic practice by noticing that the press applies a narrative structure to ambiguous events in order to create a coherent and causal sense of events.

For citizens and information consumers (which are one in the same today), it is important to develop the skill of detecting bias. Remember: Bias does not suggest that a message is false or unfair. You should apply other techniques in the Rhetorica Critical Meter to determine if a message is fallacious.

Critical Questions for Detecting Bias

1. What is the author's / speaker's socio-political position? With what social, political, or professional groups is the speaker identified?

2. Does the speaker have anything to gain personally from delivering the message?

3. Who is paying for the message? Where does the message appear? What is the bias of the medium? Who stands to gain?

4. What sources does the speaker use, and how credible are they? Does the speaker cite statistics? If so, how were the data gathered, who gathered the data, and are the data being presented fully?

5. How does the speaker present arguments? Is the message one-sided, or does it include alternative points of view? Does the speaker fairly present alternative arguments? Does the speaker ignore obviously conflicting arguments?

6. If the message includes alternative points of view, how are those views characterized? Does the speaker use positive words and images to describe his/her point of view and negative words and images to describe other points of view? Does the speaker ascribe positive motivations to his/her point of view and negative motivations to alternative points of view?

Bias in the News Media

Is the news media biased toward liberals? Yes. Is the news media biased toward conservatives? Yes. These questions and answers are uninteresting because it is possible to find evidence—anecdotal and otherwise—to "prove" media bias of one stripe or another. Far more interesting and instructive is studying the inherent, or *structural*, biases of journalism as a professional practice—especially as mediated through television. I use the word "bias" here to challenge its current use by partisan critics. A more accepted, and perhaps more accurate, term would be "frame." These are some of the professional frames that structure what journalists can see and how they can present what they see.

1. *Commercial bias*: The news media are money-making businesses. As such, they must deliver a good product to their customers to make a profit. The customers of the news media are advertisers. The most important product the news media delivers to its customers are readers or viewers. Good is de-

fined in numbers and quality of readers or viewers. The news media are biased toward conflict (re: bad news and narrative biases below) because conflict draws readers and viewers. Harmony is boring.

2. *Temporal bias*: The news media are biased toward the immediate. News is what's new and fresh. To be immediate and fresh, the news must be ever-changing even when there is little news to cover.

3. *Visual bias*: Television (and, increasingly, newspapers) is biased toward visual depictions of news. Television is nothing without pictures. Legitimate news that has no visual angle is likely to get little attention. Much of what is important in politics—policy—cannot be photographed.

4. *Bad news bias*: Good news is boring (and probably does not photograph well, either). This bias makes the world look like a more dangerous place than it really is. Plus, this bias makes politicians look far more crooked than they really are.

[T]he 24-hour news cycle—driven by the immediacy of television and the internet—creates a situation in which the job of competing never comes to a rest.

---

5. *Narrative bias*: The news media cover the news in terms of "stories" that must have a beginning, middle, and end—in other words, a plot with antagonists and protagonists. Much of what happens in our world, however, is ambiguous. The news media apply a narrative structure to ambiguous events suggesting that these events are easily understood and have clear cause-and-effect relationships. Good storytelling requires drama, and so this bias often leads journalists to add, or seek out, drama for the sake of drama. Controversy creates drama. Journalists often seek out the opinions of competing experts or officials in order to present conflict between two sides of an issue (sometimes referred to as the authority-disorder bias). Lastly, narrative bias leads many journalists to create, and then

hang on to, master narratives—set story lines with set characters who act in set ways. Once a master narrative has been set, it is very difficult to get journalists to see that their narrative is simply one way, and not necessarily the correct or best way, of viewing people and events.

6. *Status Quo bias*: The news media believe "the system works." During the "fiasco in Florida," recall that the news media were compelled to remind us that the Constitution was safe, the process was working, and all would be well. The mainstream news media never question the structure of the political system. The American way is the only way, politically and socially. In fact, the American way is news. The press spends vast amounts of time in unquestioning coverage of the process of political campaigns (but less so on the process of governance). This bias ensures that alternate points of view about how government might run and what government might do are effectively ignored.

7. *Fairness bias*: No, this is not an oxymoron. Ethical journalistic practice demands that reporters and editors be fair. In the news product this bias manifests as a contention between/among political actors (also re: narrative bias above). Whenever one faction or politician does something or says something newsworthy, the press is compelled by this bias to get a reaction from an opposing camp. This creates the illusion that the game of politics is always contentious and never cooperative. This bias can also create situations in which one faction appears to be attacked by the press. For example, politician A announces some positive accomplishment followed by the press seeking a negative comment from politician B. The point is not to disparage politician A but to be fair to politician B. When politician A is a conservative, this practice appears to be liberal bias.

8. *Expediency bias*: Journalism is a competitive, deadline-driven profession. Reporters compete among themselves for prime space or air time. News organizations compete for mar-

ket share and reader/viewer attention. And the 24-hour news cycle—driven by the immediacy of television and the internet—creates a situation in which the job of competing never comes to a rest. Add financial pressures to this mix—the general desire of media groups for profit margins that exceed what's "normal" in many other industries—and you create a bias toward reformation that can be obtained quickly, easily, and inexpensively. Need an expert/official quote (status quo bias) to balance (fairness bias) a story (narrative bias)? Who can you get on the phone fast? Who is always ready with a quote and always willing to speak (i.e. say what you need them to say to balance the story)? Who sent a press release recently? Much of deadline decision making comes down to gathering information that is readily available from sources that are well known.

Accuracy in Media claims the news media are biased toward liberal politics. Fairness & Accuracy in Media claims the news media are biased toward conservative politics. . . . But the reality is not that simple.

---

9. *Glory bias*: Journalists, especially television reporters, often assert themselves into the stories they cover. This happens most often in terms of proximity, i.e. to the locus of unfolding events or within the orbit of powerful political and civic actors. This bias helps journalists establish and maintain a cultural identity as knowledgeable insiders (although many journalists reject the notion that follows from this—that they are players in the game and not merely observers). The glory bias shows itself in particularly obnoxious ways in television journalism. News promos with stirring music and heroic pictures of individual reporters create the aura of omnipresence and omnipotence. I ascribe the use of the satellite phone to this bias. Note how often it's used in situations in which a normal video feed should be no problem to establish, e.g. a report

from Tokyo I saw recently on CNN. The jerky pictures and fuzzy sound of the satellite phone create a romantic image of foreign adventure.

Structural Bias as Theory

I have asserted that some critics of the press think of it as speaking with a unified voice with a distinct ideological bias. I have further asserted that this simplistic thinking fits the needs of ideological struggle, but is hardly useful in coming to a better understanding of what is happening in the world. For that better understanding we need a theory.

A theory offers us a model that tells us why things happen as they do. Further, a theory allows us to predict outcomes and behavior. Assertions of ideological bias do neither. While we can expect the press to demonstrate ideological biases in regard to certain issues or other localized phenomena, these and other behaviors are explained and predicted by the structural biases. Since the press sometimes demonstrates a conservative bias, asserting that the press is liberal neither predicts nor explains. Since the press sometimes demonstrates a liberal bias, asserting that the press is conservative neither predicts nor explains.

Test this for yourself. Choose a situation that is current—preferably breaking right now. For each of the structural biases listed above, write down what you would expect the press to do based on that bias. Then, complete the exercise with a concluding statement that takes into account as many of the structural biases as possible. Now, follow the situation for a few days and note how the press behaves. I think you will find that you have successfully predicted press behavior.

News Media Assumptions About Language and Discourse

Simply communicating by written or spoken words introduces bias to the message. If, as asserted earlier, there is no such thing as an objective point of view, then there cannot be objective or transparent language, i.e. a one-to-one correspondence between reality and words such that I may accurately represent reality so that you experience it as I do. Language mediates our lived experiences. And our evaluation of those experiences are reflected in our language use. Rhetoric scholar James A. Berlin once said that language is "never innocent." By this he meant that language cannot be neutral; it reflects and structures our ideologies and world views. To speak at all is to speak politically. The practice of journalism, however, accepts a very different view of language that creates serious consequences for the news consumer. Most journalists do their jobs with little or no thought given to language theory, i.e. how language works and how humans use language. Most journalists, consciously or not, accept a theory (metaphor) of language as a transparent conduit along which word-ideas are easily sent to a reader or viewer who then experiences reality as portrayed by the words.

From George Lakoff's *Moral Politics*, journalism *falsely* asserts that:

1. *Concepts are literal and nonpartisan*: The standard six-question rubric of journalism (who, what, when, where, why, how) cannot capture the complexity of issues as seen through, and expressed by, the incompatible moral systems of liberals and conservatives.

2. *Language use is neutral*: "Language is associated with a conceptual system. To use the language of a moral or political conceptual system is to use and to reinforce that conceptual system."

3. *News can be reported in neutral terms*: Not if #2 is correct. To choose a discourse is to choose a position. To attempt neutrality confuses the political concepts. Is it an "inheritance tax" or a "death tax"? What could possibly be a neutral term? To use both in the name of bal-

ance is confusing because most news articles don't have the space, and most TV treatments don't have the time, to fully explain the terms and why liberals prefer one and conservatives prefer the other. There's no time or space to explain why this language difference matters (beyond political tactics) to the formation, implementation, and evaluation of policy.

4. *Mere use of language cannot put anyone at a disadvantage*: Again, see #2.

5. *All readers and viewers share the same conceptual system*: We share the same English language, i.e. its grammar. We often do not share dialects or the denotations and connotations of concepts, lived experience, and ideologies. The statement "I am a patriotic American" means something entirely different to liberals and conservatives. That difference is more than a matter of connotation. The differences in connotation spring from different moral constructs. What the conservative means by that statement appears immoral to the liberal and vice versa.

These false assumptions by journalists, rather than overt politicking, help create the political bias news consumers often detect in news reporting. A conservative will quite naturally assert a conservative world view by using concepts in ways comfortable to conservatives. The same goes for liberals. It is often pointed out that most news reporters are Democrats or vote for Democrats. Party affiliation, however, tells us nothing about political ideology and the moral concepts that undergird it. There are conservative Democrats and liberal Republicans. Be that as it may, the ethics of journalistic practice strongly urge reporters to adopt the assumptions about language listed above and the structural biases listed above. The ethics of journalistic practice encourage journalism to adopt a (nonexistent) neutral language to mitigate any effects of ideological bias. There simply is no concerted or sustained effort to slant the news for political purposes by mainstream news outlets.

Anti-bias Crusading Is an Elitist Practice

Accuracy in Media [AIM] claims the news media are biased toward liberal politics. Fairness & Accuracy in Media [FAIR] claims the news media are biased toward conservative politics. Supporters of these views see one group as right and the other as wrong. But the reality is not that simple. Yes, AIM and FAIR each point out coverage that appears to bolster their various claims. At times, the media do seem to be biased one way or the other. What these groups don't say, however, is that their mistrust of the media is also a mistrust of the people. Those who complain most about media bias would see themselves as able to identify it and resist it. They get upset about it because they question whether the average American is able to do the same. If the average American can identify it and resist it, then there is little need to get upset about bias. The AIM and FAIR web sites are full of material to help hapless Americans avoid the cognitive ravages of the "evil" conservatives or the "slandering" liberals and their media lackeys. I believe the average American is quite capable of identifying problems with news coverage. In my opinion, crusading against political bias in the news media is an elitist practice.

6

The Transparency of the New Social Media Erases the Need for Objectivity

Mathew Ingram

Mathew Ingram is communities editor of The Globe and Mail, *a daily newspaper in Toronto and one of Canada's two national newspapers. He has been a business reporter, a stock-market columnist, an online technology writer, and a blogger for the* Globe.

The use of social media encourages journalists to be candid about their own opinions. The New York Times *and the* Washington Post *recently announced new social media policies that restrict their staffers' use of Twitter and other social media sites. The policies reflect the papers' traditional concern for the maintenance of objectivity and impartiality. In the new media environment, however, journalists are adjusting their understanding of the importance of objectivity, which may be replaced with greater transparency about the opinions of those producing the news.*

Nothing brings home the clash of cultures between "new" and "old" media like the debates over social-media policies at mainstream publications like the *New York Times* and the *Washington Post*. Earlier this year [2009], the *Times* was in the spotlight for its attempt to develop a policy on Twitter in the wake of some indiscreet twittering about internal staff meetings. Last week [September 2009] it was the *Post*'s turn:

The paper introduced a new social media policy that restricts its staffers from posting their opinions on Twitter (or any other social network), after one of its managing editors posted his thoughts about certain political issues such as health care and Congressional term limits.

The editor in question, Raju Narisetti, appeared frustrated with the moves, saying: "For flagbearers of free speech, some newsroom execs have the weirdest double standards when it comes to censoring personal views." He has since said that he agrees with the policy, however, and has cancelled his Twitter account. Other WaPo [*Washington Post*] journalists mocked the changes, meanwhile, with media reporter Howard Kurtz saying that "Under new WP guidelines on tweeting, I will now hold forth only on the weather and dessert recipes."

The guidelines . . . state that "nothing we do must call into question the impartiality of our news judgment" and highlighted "the importance of fact and objectivity, the appropriate use of language and tone, and other hallmarks of our brand of journalism." . . .

Those criticizing the newspaper's moves . . . are of the view that objectivity is ultimately impossible, and that transparency is actually a better goal.

A Negative Response

The response from some media industry observers was harsh: Rafat Ali, founder of *PaidContent* (owned by Guardian Media) said on Twitter: "I hope WaPo chokes on its own spit. New lame social media guidelines 4 journos," and CUNY [City University of New York] journalism professor and blogger Jeff Jarvis said: "*Washington Post* turns journalists into antisocial mannequins. So much for new connections to the community." Northeastern University journalism professor Dan

Kennedy said: "I would tweak WashPost Twitter policy: staffers can resume tweeting after taking advantage of company-paid lobotomy."

Journalist Amy Gahran said that "when journos pretend to have NO opinions/biases, it *undermines* their credibility," and Lisa Williams of Placeblogger.com said: "The fact that biases aren't revealed just makes fertile ground for conspiracy theories, which erode trust in journalism." . . .

From the *Washington Post*'s point of view (and that of the *New York Times*, and the *Wall Street Journal*, which issued similar rules), the maintenance of objectivity—or at least the appearance of objectivity—is the ultimate goal, and any potential benefits that stem from social media must be sacrificed in the pursuit of it. Those criticizing the newspaper's moves, however, are of the view that objectivity is ultimately impossible, and that transparency is actually a better goal. In other words, disclosure of personal views and opinions whenever and wherever possible, rather than a pretense that they don't exist.

Another Vision from Britain

In an interesting juxtaposition, just as the *Washington Post* was rushing its new social media policy out the door, the BBC's global news director was speaking to a media conference about the benefits of social media. Here's *Guardian* reporter Mercedes Bunz on Richard Sambrook's vision:

> Objectivity, he then pointed out, had always been an idea important for the news. For him it was once designed to deliver journalism that people can trust. But in the new media age transparency is what delivers trust. He stressed that news today still has to be accurate and fair, but it is as important for the readers, listeners and viewers to see how the news is produced, where the information comes from, and how it works. The emergence of news is as important as the delivering of the news itself.

Sambrook also spoke about "collaboration, openness and the culture of the link."

So does this mean that reporters should feel free to openly criticize (or support) the people or organizations they are writing about? Some are afraid that, in that kind of world, everything will become opinion and no one will care about the facts any more—*Technology Review* editor Jason Pontin said on Twitter that someone "has to be in the business of describing what is factually known, before the rhetoric begins."

[A] smart newspaper or media outlet should realize that using social media to connect with readers . . . is a positive thing, rather than something to be feared and protected against.

For what it's worth, I don't think it has to be a binary choice. I think a smart reporter or writer won't say things that would damage his or her credibility, either on Twitter or anywhere else. (*Times* editor Bill Keller effectively said the same thing during the fuss over the *Times'* policy.) At the same time, however, a smart newspaper or media outlet should realize that using social media to connect with readers—even if that means embracing more transparency than it is typically used to—is a positive thing, rather than something to be feared and protected against.

7

Verification Is More Important Than Objectivity

Jack Shafer

Jack Shafer is a writer for the online magazine Slate. *He edits and writes the column "Press Box."*

The employers of recently fired journalists Octavia Nasr and David Weigel have defended their actions, saying that Nasr and Weigel created the appearance of bias by their candid expression of personal opinion via social media—Twitter and a private e-mail list, respectively. But it is wrong to suggest that journalists do not have biases, or to imply that biases have a negative impact on the work of journalists. In fact, bias is an inevitable part of every kind of inquiry. What should be unbiased is the method of seeking out and verifying information in order to draw conclusions.

Speak your mind, lose your job is the lesson I'm taking away from yesterday's [July 7, 2010] sacking of CNN senior editor Octavia Nasr. Nasr, who had worked for the network for 20 years, tweeted this upon the death of Shiite cleric Grand Ayatollah Mohammed Hussein Fadlallah:

> Sad to hear of the passing of Sayyed Mohammed Hussein Fadlallah . . . One of Hezbollah's giants I respect a lot.

Nasr promptly published a mea culpa, blaming the 140-character brevity of Twitter for her "error of judgment." She regretted having tried to express complex views about Fadlallah's life's work in a simplistic forum. Then, she spent 3,964 characters trying to clarify her tweet and save her job. No luck. An internal CNN memo obtained by the *New York Times* stated that Nasr was sent packing because "her credibility" had "been compromised."

The dumping of Nasr follows the defenestration of *Washington Post* blogger Dave Weigel, whose resignation was accepted on June 25 [2010] after intemperate comments he had made about conservatives in a private listserv were leaked to *FishbowlDC* and the *Daily Caller*.

Weigel's acerbic listserv comments, some made before he went to work for the *Post*, bad-mouthed some of the very conservatives he had been hired to cover. Weigel called upon Matt Drudge to torch himself, labeled Newt Gingrich an "amoral blowhard," and otherwise disparaged conservatives. Weigel, too, has apologized, saying he regrets his rudeness and "hubris." In an *Esquire.com* piece published today, Weigel writes that he "had a bad habit of using [the listserv] as an idea latrine." (Idea Latrine would be a great name for a band.)

[B]iases shouldn't be thought of as invasive weeds, choking the garden, but as nutrients. The job of a journalist is to gather evidence, test it, and come to conclusions wherever feasible.

In the wake of Weigel's departure, his ultimate boss, *Post* Executive Editor Marcus Brauchli, offered this mind-bending statement to *Post* reporter Howard Kurtz. "[W]e can't have any tolerance for the perception that people are conflicted or bring a bias to their work. . . . There's abundant room on our Web site for a wide range of viewpoints, and we should be transparent about everybody's viewpoint." [Ellipsis in the original.]

Brauchli seems to be saying that *Post* reporters *can* bring biases to their journalism, just as long as they don't reveal them. But the post-ellipsis part of his statement appears to contradict that reading, because if everybody were to suddenly become transparent about their viewpoints at the *Post* perception of bias would rise, crest, and surely swamp readers. And Brauchli can't possibly want that.

Brauchli's confusion over where reporters should stow their personal luggage—in a dark and locked closet or in the vestibule where anybody can pick through it—goes to the center of the two controversies. That journalists have opinions and express them in private and sometimes (to their frequent regret) in public should come as no shocker. If you prick them, they bleed, too.

But such biases shouldn't be thought of as invasive weeds, choking the garden, but as nutrients. The job of a journalist is to gather evidence, test it, and come to conclusions wherever feasible. Such an enterprise is impossible to undertake without biases. Indeed, like scientific inquiries, almost every new story begins with some sort of bias or hunch or leaning. A reporter or an editor thinks *this* story is more promising or interesting than *that* story, therefore they agree to pursue it. But without reporting both stories—or every possible story, which is impossible—how can the editor and reporter really know which was the "right" story to assign? They can't. They can only trust their biases.

Biases may be necessary for the production of quality journalism, but as anybody who has ever listened to a blowhard or read a listserv or Twitter feed knows, they're not sufficient. Nor is objectivity the key, or what passes for objectivity in journalism these days. As Tom Rosenstiel and Bill Kovach explain in their 2001 book, *The Elements of Journalism*, the key element is *verification*. Lamenting the loss of the original meaning of "objectivity" in journalism, the duo writes:

When the concept originally evolved, it was not meant to imply that journalists were free of bias. Quite the contrary. The term began to appear as part of journalism early in the last century, particularly in the 1920s, out of a growing recognition that journalists were full of bias, often unconsciously. Objectivity called for journalists to develop a consistent method of testing information—a transparent approach to evidence—precisely so that personal and culture biases would not undermine their work.

The journalistic *method* was the thing that was supposed to be objective, not the journalist, a method that depended on *verification* of results and findings. Rosenstiel and Kovach complain about how the old journalism of verification has been "overrun" by the new journalism of assertion that we consume on TV and radio. They also bellyache about the neutral voice adopted by unscrupulous journalists who want to appear objective when they're completely in the tank for somebody. This, they write, is a "form of deception." In my book, this kind of deception—and not shooting off your mouth—should be a firing offense.

Which brings us back to Weigel and Nasr. To the best of my knowledge, neither journalist has been criticized for producing substandard or otherwise shoddy work for their network or newspaper. Both appear to be committed to the journalism of verification, although I'm more confident about vouching for Weigel's work, which I know well, than Nasr's, which I don't. Weigel's jerkiness on a private listserv doesn't bother me much at all. If you were to purge the *Post* newsroom of every reporter who had been a jerk sometime in his career, you'd be facing an acre of empty desks. In fact, jerkiness was one of the attributes that I used to look for in a candidate when I was on the management side of the editorial divide.

That Weigel's bad manners bothered his *Post* bosses so much that they felt compelled to accept his resignation speaks poorly for the paper. That CNN walked Nasr off the plank because she expressed a smidgeon of "respect" for a Hezbollah-supporting cleric in a tweet speaks of cowardice.

The work is the thing. Until somebody can show me shoddy journalism by Weigel and Nasr, I'll defend them. Nobody should be sacked to pacify the nitpickers.

8

The Mainstream Media Are Biased in Favor of the Democratic Party

Dan Whitfield

Dan Whitfield is a British writer living in Washington, D.C.

Studies have shown that the mainstream media have a history of being biased toward the Democratic Party. For so many members of the media, to favor the Democrats is a cause for concern. However, conservatives have in significant measure created the problem themselves by confining themselves to talk radio, conservative magazines, and message boards. Also, those conservatives who have worked in journalism have tended to embrace partisan controversy and show little concern to preserve the appearance of objectivity. There is a great need in the mainstream media for high quality conservative journalism.

After a bruising primary season, the GOP [Grand Old Party or the Republican Party] establishment is trying to come to terms with a Tea Party movement that enjoys the loyalty of thousands of activists across the country. Tales of infighting are already starting to circulate. But while the moderate and conservative wings of the Republican Party are sniping at each other, they can at least agree on something: the mainstream media remains overwhelmingly biased in favor of the Democratic Party and President Barack Obama.

But while Republicans have defined the problem, they have failed to provide a solution.

Complaints about media bias are not mere sour grapes—conservatives have reason to be upset. The Project for Excellence in Journalism published a study in 2008 demonstrating how stories covering Republican presidential candidate John McCain were largely negative, in contrast to more positive stories on then-Senator Obama. Ordinary voters are aware of this imbalance. Prior to the 2008 presidential election, polls of likely voters showed just 9% thought professional journalists wanted Senator McCain to be elected president.

Voters Are Immune to Bias

Conservatives, however, should beware exaggerating the problem. As far back as 1986, professors S. Robert Lichter, Stanley Rothman and Linda S. Lichter found that journalists preferred Democratic to Republican candidates by a large margin. That did not stop President Ronald Reagan from winning two elections. Likewise, more recent surveys have shown media professionals are more supportive of left-wing candidates over conservatives. Hence the candidacies of Michael Dukakis, Al Gore, and John Kerry were, according to such sources as the Freedom Forum, supported by the majority of journalists. Yet each of these candidates failed to be elected president. Such evidence should help convince irate conservatives that American voters are largely immune to alleged media bias.

Complaining about the media, while steadfastly refusing to engage with it, will not cure the ills manifest in American journalism.

Even so, the data suggests a troubling trend. The US Constitution safeguarded the principle of a free press, and to see it controlled by huge majorities of like-minded people is a cause for concern. While great strides have been made in racial and sexual diversity, major newsrooms show a stunning lack of diversity in political thought. Even the most trenchant liberal must concede that such a situation is alarming.

But if conservatives have grasped the problem, they have failed to find a suitable response. The overwhelmingly positive coverage of the left is not the fault of any liberal conspiracy. It is the fault of the conservative movement itself.

Complaining Won't Help

After years of complaining about declining standards in journalism, the response of conservatives has been woeful. Conservatives have resorted to retreating into their strongholds: talk radio, conservative magazines, and various online message boards where they complain to one another at length. Such a move insulates conservatives from larger media outlets at a time when their message needs to be heard. Complaining about the media, while steadfastly refusing to engage with it, will not cure the ills manifest in American journalism.

Mark Levin [a political commentator], for example, had excoriated segments of the media for questioning the background of Christine O'Donnell, the newly-minted Republican candidate in the [2010] Delaware Senate race. But he misses the point—in questioning O'Donnell's bona fides, the media is not lashing out at her political beliefs, but rather asking her to account for troubling past deeds. If O'Donnell does not address these valid concerns through the media, doubts about her self-efficacy will continue.

In response to this increased media interest, Sarah Palin, former governor of Alaska, has advised O'Donnell to "speak through Fox News." While Fox remains a center of high journalistic integrity, O'Donnell would be foolish to follow such advice—she would open herself to charges that she is hiding from the wider media.

This is precisely the foolish course of action chartered by Sharron Angle, the Republican Senate candidate in Nevada. who last month [August 2010] lashed out at the media for not "asking the questions we want to answer." Such behavior smacks of immaturity. Another Republican out West, Governor Jan Brewer of Arizona, has refused to participate in any more debates with her Democratic challenger after her famous on-air meltdown two weeks ago. It is hard for conservatives to ask the media for fairness when GOP [Grand Old Party or the Republican Party] candidates behave in such a manner.

Conservative Journalists Revel in Controversy

A second difficulty is that those conservatives who work in journalism seldom make any pretense of objectivity. They revel in controversy. Right-wing commentators are therefore reduced to the status of token conservative, a blinkered partisan which liberals can lampoon with ease. Conservatives should remember that America is poorly served by replacing a liberal bias with a conservative one.

When conservatives bring their politics and grievances into the newsrooms of various media, they reinforce the perception of many on the left: those on the right are short sighted, easily angered, and apt to confuse the difference between glib punditry and hard-nosed journalism.

Recently, there have been encouraging signs of change within the conservative movement. Groups like the National Journalism Center and the Leadership Institute are offering training programs, internships, and scholarship funds designed to give aspiring journalists the edge in a highly competitive job market. Hopefully such moves will reverse the decline in journalistic standards.

Liberal editorializing skewed the narrative of the 2008 election. But the situation is not beyond rescue. The perennial hero of the right—Ronald Reagan—was, after all, the Great Communicator. By actively engaging with the mainstream media, conservatives will start to redress the imbalance. But if conservatives simply resort to the ways of old, offering the media either no conservative response or else a slew of incensed blowhards, liberal bias will go unchallenged. If conservatives do not set about addressing this challenge with sincerity and maturity, they will do a disservice both to their cause and their country.

9

The Mainstream Media Tilt Toward the Republicans

Jonathan Weiler

Jonathan Weiler, a professor at the University of North Carolina Chapel Hill, is a contributor to The Huffington Post.

A Media Matters study conducted during the George W. Bush administration showed that there is a strong tilt toward the political right on Sunday morning talk shows, and some have suggested that extremist conservative politicians receive far more media attention than is merited. This is the result of efforts by the media to achieve "balance," but it actually results in a kind of journalistic affirmative action quota system that distorts the news. Unwarranted amounts of coverage of Newt Gingrich, a former Republican Speaker of the House of Representatives who served in the 1990s, is an example of this.

What is the purpose of a news organization? Is it to inform the public? Or is it to provide affirmative action opportunities to the right-wing?

OK, I won't keep you in suspense. I'd like to suggest that it's the latter, and that the new Exhibit A is [former Speaker of the House] Newt Gingrich.

A few years ago, during W. [President George W. Bush] time, Paul Waldman conducted a couple of studies for Media Matters in which he showed the strong rightward tilt of the Sunday morning political talk shows. Among the lame responses he got from the networks was that, well, the Republicans are in power now, and we have to talk to the people in power.

But "a deep and largely unconscious conservative media bias," as [political commentator] E.J. Dionne has called it, has continued to pervade our information environment, persisting right through landslide defeats for Republicans in 2006 and 2008 and has shown itself immune to the relative political fortunes of Democrats and Republicans. And it has allowed a steady stream of extremists, including [Congresswoman Michele] Bachmann, [former vice presidential candidate Sarah] Palin, [conservative radio and television host Glenn] Beck, [conservative radio talk show host Bush] Limbaugh, [political activist] Liz Cheney, the would-be Quran burner from Florida and more to garner copious media attention.

A Persistent Bias for the Political Right

What can explain the persistence of this tilt regardless of the relative popularity of the American right, or the political composition of our governing bodies?

For my money, the best explanation is that, for all their complaints about affirmative action, the right-wing is benefiting greatly from what can best be described as an affirmative action media policy, otherwise called "balance." In its mindless pursuit of such balance, the media has created an intellectual quota system, a particularly invidious form of affirmative action. This policy has ensured that no matter how wrong, incoherent, uninformative or unpopular they are—the first three of which ought to be the basic metrics for merit-based access to media platforms—right-wing blowhards will continue to get more than equal air time to propagate their nonsense.

Which brings us to Newt Gingrich. Yes, he is a former Speaker of the House. So was Tom Foley and I defy anyone to argue that, no matter how hard he tried, he could ever get his mug to litter the airwaves the way Gingrich's does. Claiming someone is newsworthy is simply circular reasoning. Gingrich is receiving lots of attention because news organizations are giving him lots of attention. Does anyone want to argue seriously that the public as a whole is clamoring to hear what Newt Gingrich has to say? About anything?

It can't be that Gingrich is uniquely positioned to provide informed, cogent commentary on public affairs. Just a small smattering of the incredibly stupid things that Gingrich has uttered in the past eighteen months:

- he's compared all of Islam to Nazism

- asserted that the US should have more or less the same level of religious freedom as Saudi Arabia

- warned of the specter of [Venezuelan president] Hugo Chavez wanting to destroy America and, therefore, criticized President [Barack] Obama for "showing weakness" by shaking hands with him (as an aside, how could any one possibly project more weakness than Gingrich does when he proposes that, in effect, we should fear interaction with the leader of Venezuela? Pathetic.)

- endorsed a truly moronic and racially inflammatory article by [author and public speaker] Dinesh D'Souza (which argued that Obama was living out the "anti-colonialist" fantasies of his Kenyan father at the expense of America)—by calling it the "most profound insight I have read in the last six years about Barack Obama."

The Tip of the Iceberg

Of course, this is only the tip of the iceberg of Gingrich's repeated, relentless distortion of fact, inflaming of public sentiment and generally malign and ill-informed "contribution" to our public life.

Yes, I know that Gingrich is now making noises about running for President in 2012 and that recent polling shows that he's fairly popular with the Republican base. But two points:

1) I will bet dollars to donuts that Gingrich ultimately has no shot of winning the Republican nomination in 2012 (much as I would love that outcome).

2) I think it's fair to say that a central factor in Gingrich's being able even to consider running is the absurd level of media attention he's received since Obama became president. In other words, to the extent that he's a remotely viable candidate, this is a function of the attention media have given him. His high profile is an effect of media coverage, not a cause of it.

So if you ever hear a Gingrich lecture about the evils of affirmative action, you can treat it with the same level of seriousness you would a Gingrich lecture on, say, family values and marital fidelity.

10

Bias in the Business Media Contributed to the Financial Crisis

Dean Starkman

Dean Starkman covers the business press for the Columbia Journalism Review.

Readers, including investors and citizens, need journalists who will call attention to problems in the business community before they become crises. However, it is unlikely that the business press will produce this kind of journalism in the future. Shrinking budgets and staffs at media outlets, lack of management support for investigative stories, and an increasing "insider" focus among business journalists caused the business press to miss the subprime mortgage crisis of 2007 and 2008, and since then conditions have only become worse.

For casual readers of business coverage—that is most of us—the past 18 months [July 2007 to December 2008] have been a crash course in things we never knew existed but that, we are told, have already done us all irreparable harm. Not only are the problems catastrophic, goes the somewhat frustrating message, but it is already too late to do anything about them—other, that is, than pay for them.

In looking back on how we got here, the business press assumes a tone of rueful omniscience, as in this late-2007 *New*

York Times piece on regulatory laxity, under Alan Greenspan [Federal Reserve chairman from 1987 to 2006]: "Had officials bothered to look, frightening clues of the coming crisis were available." Of course, the clues the *Times* cites in the very next sentence—the ceaseless research of the North Carolina-based Center for Responsible Lending—were available had anyone bothered to look. So, a reader might well ask, why didn't the media?

I worked as a *Wall Street Journal* staff writer for eight years ending in December 2004 and now critique the business media full time at the *Columbia Journalism Review*. I'll attest that business journalists as a rule are as smart, sophisticated, and plugged-in as they seem. And yet that army of professional business reporters—an estimated 9,000 or so nationwide in print alone—for all practical purposes missed the biggest story on the beat. Why?

Around the same time, the drip of newsroom cuts became a deluge—in all, newspapers lost 13,000 jobs last year—and business news hasn't been spared.

In October, Howard Kurtz, the *Washington Post* media critic, rounded up the opinions of a few practitioners. Some bravely took the blame ("We all failed," ventured CNBC's Charlie Gasparino), but the majority chose to blame the audience: "If we had written stories in late 2000 saying this whole thing's going to collapse," said *Fortune* managing editor Andy Serwer, "people would have said, 'Ha ha, maybe,' and gone about their business." Ditto Marcus Brauchli, a top *Wall Street Journal* editor during the bubble before taking over last July as executive editor of the *Washington Post*: "I regret that when I was at the *Journal*, we didn't keep the focus on some of these questions, including the possible moral hazard posed by the structure of Fannie Mae and Freddie Mac. These are really difficult issues to convey to a popular audience."

There was a handful of heroes at the major publications who tried to get the word out. But the good, hard-hitting, arm's-length stories will have to be compared to what else was gushing out of the 30-inch business-news drainpipe—those Citigroup earnings stories, those edgy-yet-flattering profiles of Merrill Lynch's Stan O'Neal, Lehman Brothers' Dick Fuld, et al., the pieces noting how Countrywide Financial's Angelo Mozilo liked to dress well, etc., not to mention the Home Depot marketing stories, the personal finance columns, and all the cheerleading and *Flip That House* fluff that diverted resources from the real task at hand. What was really the business-press message? It was certainly not that mortgage lenders and Wall Street had linked up to flood the market with defective products.

An Industry in Decline

It is true, though, that the circumstances conspired to make the press' job harder—much harder—than usual. Consider, first, the industry's own failing financial health. In 1998, the New York Times Company's newspaper segment generated profit margins of 24 percent—about the sector's average then—according to John Morton, a leading industry analyst. The comparable figure for the first half of 2008 is 8.5 percent. This so-called margin compression affects the newspaper industry generally, extends to the magazine business, and has led to a collapse in stock prices across the board. The Times Company traded for $50 a share as recently as 2002. Today, it's around $10 and still considered a "sell" by some analysts. Its market capitalization—stock price multiplied by the number of shares outstanding—is $1.5 billion, half of which is its stake in its new Eighth Avenue headquarters. The value the market places on its prospects is basically zero.

The demise of the mainstream media, especially newspapers, has been forecast for decades, but the years following the tech wreck of 2000—the period of the housing bubble—

opened a new, defining chapter. The most shocking plunge in values came, Morton says, around mid-2007, just about the time the credit crisis burst into full view. For instance, the market capitalization of the Journal Register Company, publisher of the *New Haven Register* and hundreds of smaller papers, has fallen more than 99 percent since the start of 2007—long before, it's worth remembering, the credit crisis made business flameouts commonplace. In newspapering, it was the business model itself that fell apart.

Around the same time, the drip of newsroom cuts became a deluge—in all, newspapers lost 13,000 jobs last year—and business news hasn't been spared. Chris Roush, director of the Carolina Business News Initiative at the University of North Carolina-Chapel Hill, estimates that the number of print business reporters around the country has fallen 25 percent since 2000, to 9,000. Business pages of major regional papers have been especially hard-hit: Since 2004, the *Washington Post* business staff has lost 30 of its top reporters. The *Los Angeles Times* has lost at least 15, leaving it with a total of around 50. Yes, we've seen the launch of a brand-new TV news channel, Fox Business News—but that's just another competitor chasing the same shrinking advertising market. And in any case, no one should be under the illusion that TV business news, with its gaze narrowly focused on the gyrations of the stock market concerns, could ever have offered the kind of long-term warnings that would have saved its viewers' nest eggs. Newspapers were supposed to be different.

Gravy Train Days Are Gone

When I arrived at the *Journal* as a staff writer in the law group, in 1996, Dow Jones' & Co.'s market cap was more than $4 billion. That was back when the paper *had* a law group, and a Philadelphia bureau, a Pittsburgh bureau, and several Canadian bureaus. It also used to have a cafeteria and a guy who pushed a coffee cart around the floor twice a day. Dow

Jones was never a corporate giant, but it was a big, sturdy company, about the same size as many of the Wall Street firms it covered. (Morgan Stanley was about a $5 billion company in the mid-1990s.) You can argue that size doesn't matter; all I can say is that it made for a confident, freewheeling environment, where the staff was encouraged to take a chance once in a while, maybe even think big. A *Journal* reporter had swagger.

Time-consuming investigations were undertaken at the reporter's own risk: If a lead didn't pan out—no matter why—it hit your productivity numbers, putting your career in peril.

Penelope Muse Abernathy, a *Journal* executive until 2006 and now a professor of media economics at Chapel Hill, says the late-1990s economic expansion fed a virtuous cycle in which profits funded good journalism that would attract more readers and profit. "If you were a business reporter, these were the gravy train days," she says.

Indeed. I rode in black cars, lunched at all the places you read about, and more than once flew across the country to report a 1,200-word story. Every year, Dow Jones dropped an amount equivalent to 15 percent of my gross pay into a pension account, just like that. When I picked up the *Journal* on my doorstep in the late 1990s, the Monday edition was the size of the Brooklyn phone book.

But not for long.

Dow Jones made particular strategic missteps that need not trouble us here, but those merely left it somewhat more unprepared than other media companies when the tech meltdown ushered in a severe advertising recession, one made permanent by the rise of the Internet. By the time I left at the end of 2004, the newsroom had gone through at least three rounds of layoffs, all white-knuckle, morale-crushing affairs. Benefits were cut to the point that the once-gung-ho staff took to picketing around a giant inflatable rat. Office politics became Byzantine, and productivity demands on the newsroom—more, faster—grew ever more pronounced. Time-consuming investigations were undertaken at the reporter's own risk: If a lead didn't pan out—no matter why—it hit your productivity numbers, putting your career in peril. This wasn't subtle stuff.

The paper, despite occasional bright spots, became rote, formulaic, dull. The *Journal's* weakened condition, financially and journalistically, cleared the way for Rupert Murdoch's News Corporation to buy it in 2007. Since then, the new owner's experimentation—more political news, cutting back the copy desk, revamping sections—has not helped the journalism. The paper has done some fine work, but in no sense did it dominate the crisis story as the *Journal* dominated core financial stories in the past.

Just as financial news outlets were weakening, regulators were also abandoning the field, leaving business reporters starved of the investigative leads they rely on.

Confrontation and Muckraking Were Not in Vogue

The disintegration of the financial media's own financial underpinnings could not have come at a worse time. Low morale, lost expertise, and constant cutbacks, especially in investigative reporting—these are not conditions that produce an appetite for confrontation and muckraking. In 2002, the *Times'* Gretchen Morgenson won a Pulitzer for beat reporting on Wall Street, beating single-handedly, in the view of some, the entire *Journal* staff.

Jesse Eisinger, a former financial columnist for the *Journal* and now a senior writer for *Portfolio*, says the paper, like business journalism generally, clung to outdated formulas. Wall

Street coverage tilted toward personality-driven stories, not deconstructing balance sheets or figuring out risks. Stocks were the focus, when the problems were brewing in derivatives. "We were following the old model," he says.

The Failure of Regulatory Agencies Played a Role

But it wasn't just the media abdicating their watchdog role: Just as financial news outlets were weakening, regulators were also abandoning the field, leaving business reporters starved of the investigative leads they rely on. Back in the 1980s, a great deal of tough Wall Street coverage was driven by the aggressive work of prosecutors and the Securities and Exchange Commission (SEC). But then came the [Bill] Clinton-era push toward deregulation that reached its extremes during the [George W.] Bush administration as the federal government unceremoniously pulled the finance cops off the beat. For a time [New York attorney general] Eliot Spitzer filled the void with his aggressive prosecution of Wall Street misdeeds, but for the most part, covering financial corruption without regulators was like trying to clap with one hand.

Take the Federal Trade Commission [FTC]. In 2002, the agency announced a then-record $240 million predatory lending settlement involving Citigroup's giant subprime units, and covering no fewer than 2 million customers. Since then the FTC has brought no major consumer lending cases. Zero. The last such case brought by the Office of the Comptroller of the Currency, against Providian National Bank, came in 2000.

The haplessness of the SEC under Chairman Christopher Cox is now widely recognized as a major contributor to the collapse. But the commission's passivity also hamstrung Wall Street reporters: It is worth remembering that prior to the Enron, WorldCom, Adelphia, and Tyco scandals earlier this decade, the SEC had already opened formal investigations into each doomed company—forcing disclosures that tipped off investors, yes, but also providing road maps and official cover to the financial press. (The problems at Enron, a special case, were first uncovered by a short seller, who tipped off reporters.)

Contrast that with the most recent disasters: Bear Stearns, Lehman Brothers, AIG, Fannie Mae, and Freddie Mac had all collapsed before the SEC had even launched an investigation. The spectacle of Lehman employees carrying out boxes of records—on television!—was too much for Jonathan Weil, a Bloomberg columnist who is known for breaking an early Enron story in 2000 while at the *Journal*. In a column last September [2009], he wrote "Is there anybody left in the government with a pulse? Where's the yellow police tape? How about a cease-and-desist order to prevent document destruction? Can anyone give me a good reason why Lehman offices shouldn't be treated as a crime scene now?"

But the regulatory absence only goes so far as an excuse for the press, says Michael Hudson, who began reporting on subprimes in the 1990s at the *Roanoke Times* and joined the *Journal* in 2006. He's now with the Center for Responsible Lending. "It's true the federal regulators disappeared," Hudson says. "But there were lots of state regulators who were going after this in a big way, lots of people on the ground, lawyers, consumer advocates, scholars, who saw what was happening, and the press didn't give them much attention."

A Trade-off Between Access and Scrutiny

In May 1990, the *Wall Street Journal* published "The Reckoning," a devastating, 7,000-word account by Susan Faludi, then a staff writer, of the human toll wrought by the leveraged buyout of the Safeway grocery chain. It is safe to say that that piece, which tied the Safeway LBO to workers' suicides, heart attacks, and more, would never be proposed, let alone published, today.

Faludi's article was distinguished by more than its scope and length. It also took on a practice that at the time was at the very heart of Wall Street's business model, not to mention one of the preeminent firms of the era, Kohlberg Kravis Roberts & Co. It then expanded the story's scope to take into account the social costs of high finance. Similarly, the *Journal's* Alix Freedman took on the tobacco industry at the height of its power in 1996, when she won a Pulitzer for stories exposing how ammonia additives heighten nicotine's potency.

Increasingly, business coverage has addressed its audience as investors rather than citizens, a subtle but powerful shift in perspective that has led to some curious choices.

By contrast, in the past few years, business-news outlets, increasingly burdened financially, less confident editorially, competing ever more fiercely among themselves, torn by the tradeoff between access and scrutiny, have slowly given away their sense of perspective. The result was an insiders' conversation—journalism that, while well executed on Wall Street's terms, in the end missed the point. There have been exceptions—a preliminary list would include Shawn Tully at *Fortune,* John Hechinger and others at the *Journal,* Mara Der Hovanesian at *BusinessWeek,* Diana Henriques and others at the *New York Times,* and Scott Reckard at the *LA Times.* But to this day, and even after the collapse, the most complete accounts of the mortgage mess have been provided not by the mainstream business press, but by *This American Life's* "Giant Pool of Money," and *Chain of Blame,* a book published last year by reporters for the *Orange County Register* and *National Mortgage News.*

Over the past decade, business news has become ever more inward looking, more incremental, and more specialized. In covering Merrill Lynch, for instance, news outlets focused on Stan O'Neal's hard-charging style, but entirely from a perspective of whether it would help Merrill shareholders. A *Fortune* headline from 2004 read, "Stan O'Neal may be the toughest—some say the most ruthless—CEO in America. Merrill Lynch couldn't be luckier to have him." There was no exploration, in *Fortune* or elsewhere, of Merrill's huge push into subprimes until after O'Neal was ousted in 2007.

The Audience: Investors or Citizens?

Increasingly, business coverage has addressed its audience as investors rather than citizens, a subtle but powerful shift in perspective that has led to some curious choices. The *Journal*, for example, at times seemed to strain to find someone other than Wall Street to blame for the mortgage mess: A December 2007 story announced that borrower fraud "goes a long way toward explaining why mortgage defaults and foreclosures are rocking financial institutions," though no such evidence exists. Another *Journal* story last March accused "about half" of foreclosed-upon borrowers of trashing their homes. The source for the "half" bit: a PR firm working for real estate clients. *Forbes*, meanwhile, in a misbegotten investigation last March of Martin Eakes, the head of the Center for Responsible Lending and one of the few heroes of the subprime mess, suggested Eakes had fought to ban abusive lending in order to help the tiny nonprofit credit union he runs. Seriously.

"It's much easier to write a story saying something is a bubble than saying it's a fraud," . . . "If business-news organizations want to be taken seriously, they need to invest in investigative journalism."

Competition has only exacerbated this narrowing of vision. Mergers-and-acquisition [M&A] coverage rose from its place as one beat among many to a full-fledged obsession generating multiple stand-alone sections and publications. But no matter how titillating, deal stories are of limited relevance to most readers, and dependent entirely on the good graces of Wall Street sources. The rise of M&A coverage represents the triumph of Wall Street insiderism. It is the opposite of Faludi's vision. Significantly, M&A has become a business-press career launching pad: Andrew Ross Sorkin, who writes the *Times'* DealBook column, and former *Wall Street Journal* M&A reporter Nik Deogun are among the field's superstars.

Another insider obsession is outsize personalities in the corner office: Coverage of Citigroup produced reams of profiles of its influential former chief, Sandy Weill, his successor, Chuck Prince, and his protégé-turned-rival, Jaime Dimon, but precious little about Citigroup's role in bringing subprime lending from the mortgage industry's margins into the mainstream. It was left to Hudson, then freelancing for the 3,000-circulation *Southern Exposure*, to tell that story (and win a Polk Award).

Personality profiles, critical as they may be, are comfortably within the narrowing business-press discourse. Plus they're a lot easier, and less risky, than investigations—and it's that part of business journalism that has been allowed to wither, says Katie Benner, a *Fortune* writer. "It's much easier to write a story saying something is a bubble than saying it's a fraud," she notes. "If business-news organizations want to be taken seriously, they need to invest in investigative journalism." Needless to say, chances for that look slim right now—but it is more than just a question of resources. Predatory lending happened in plain sight; it didn't take a muckraker to see what was wrong. Yet business journalism kept its blinders on, played it safe, fixated on stock market concerns, and allowed its BS detector to atrophy just when it was needed most.

Sure, there has been, and will be, excellent retrospective work—similar to the *Journal*'s 2002 look back on the Enron-WorldCom-Tyco period, which won a Pulitzer, but in my view was akin to kicking the wreckage after the plane had crashed. This kind of "explanatory" reporting is by definition too late. It is a lower form of journalism than probing coverage before the fact, which is the hardest to do but in the end what readers—investors, citizens—really need. Who will blow the whistle on the next disaster in the making? Where's the next subprime mess? Barring a major reordering of resources and priorities, don't count on the business media to find out. "The press were kind of prisoners of respectability," Hudson says. "With exceptions, they really want official sources; they want official approval; they don't want to be too out front. They do a good job after the fact, but not beforehand, when it counts."

11

Business Media Bias Did Not Contribute to the Financial Crisis

Chris Roush

Chris Roush is the Walter E. Hussman Sr. Distinguished Scholar in Business Journalism at the University of North Carolina at Chapel Hill and the author of Profits and Losses: Business Journalism and Its Role in Society. *He has worked as a business journalist for* BusinessWeek, Bloomberg News, *the* Atlanta Journal-Constitution, *the* Tampa Tribune, *and the* Sarasota Herald-Tribune.

As the financial crisis of 2007 and 2008 intensified, critics pointed fingers at the financial press, arguing that business journalists failed to expose the dangerous practices connected with subprime lending, adjustable rate loans, and credit derivatives. However, a review of articles published in months and even years leading up to the scandal shows that business journalists wrote in detail, and often repetitively, about the risks involved. In the midst of a bull market, at a time when many were benefiting from the business practices in question, there was very little support for critical voices and perspectives.

In the early weeks of October [2008], as the American financial crisis intensified, everyone from former Lehman Brothers CEO Richard Fuld to *Advertising Age* media critic Simon

Dumenco took shots at the business press, pummeling its reporters and editors for failing to anticipate the looming economic collapse.

"Of course, just as we're getting more self-pity than humility from Wall Street these days, we're not exactly getting much in the way of mea culpas from the financial press," Dumenco wrote on September 29 [2008]. "Nobody's really been stepping up to the plate to say, 'With our woefully incomplete and often shamefully gullible reporting on the murky financial underpinnings of the real-estate bubble, we let our readers and/or viewers down.'"

A Day Late and Dollars Short

In an October 6 [2008] story titled "Press May Own a Share in Financial Mess," *Washington Post* media writer Howard Kurtz added, "As in the savings-and-loan scandal of the late 1980s, the press was a day late and several dollars short."

And Marketwatch.com media columnist Jon Friedman, a longtime business journalist, complained about recent business coverage, particularly during a press conference announcing Bank of America's purchase of struggling Merrill Lynch. Friedman wrote: "With all the carnage, you might expect to see a pinstripe lynch mob of sorts encounter the two chief executives. But the media were so polite and deferential to the two CEOs, they behaved as if the press conference were a victory lap for the financial services industry."

The business media in 2008 serve as a welcome scapegoat for those who simply want to ignore their own culpability in the financial meltdown. But it's a bad rap. Gone since the tech bubble burst in 2000 are the flattering CEO profiles and the touting of Internet companies with no revenue. The business media have done yeoman's work during the past decade-plus to expose wrongdoing in corporate America. In fact, a review of the top business publications in the country shows that they blanketed the major issues, from subprime loans to adjustable-rate mortgages to credit derivatives, that caused so much economic pain.

As far back as 1994, Fortune *magazine's Carol Loomis predicted that derivatives could be "a villain, or even the villain, in some financial crisis that sweeps the world."*

"I take umbrage at the notion that financial journalists have let us down," says Sarah Bartlett, who runs the urban and business journalism programs at the City University of New York's Graduate School of Journalism. "It's just not true," adds Bartlett, a former assistant managing editor at *Business-Week* and business reporter at the *New York Times.*

Business Media Were Not Dazzled

The problem isn't that the business media were dazzled by soaring real-estate prices and Wall Street profits and failed to see rot beneath the surface. Rather, it was that government regulators and the general public weren't paying attention.

And the warning signs were plentiful:

As far back as 1994, *Fortune* magazine's Carol Loomis predicted that derivatives could be "a villain, or even the villain, in some financial crisis that sweeps the world." The complicated investments she mentioned are those we've seen unravel this year.

The *Wall Street Journal*'s aggressive coverage of government-based lenders Fannie Mae and Freddie Mac dates back nearly a decade. In 2004, one piece in the *Journal* compared Fannie Mae to Enron and WorldCom, two companies that crashed and burned the last time business journalists were blamed for an economic downturn.

Back in 2007, under the headline "Mortgages May Be Messier Than You Think," Gretchen Morgenson of the *New York Times* wrote, "As is often the case, only after fiery markets burn out do we see the risks that buyers ignore and sellers play down." Her colleagues Diana Henriques and Floyd Norris exposed shady lending to military personnel and shaky accounting practices, respectively, in the past five years.

Washington Post columnist Steven Pearlstein has been warning of financial trouble for years. On August 1, 2007, in a column titled "Credit Markets' Weight Puts Economy on Shaky Ground," Pearlstein wrote, "This financial engineering has encouraged debt to be piled on debt, making the system more susceptible to a meltdown if credit suddenly becomes more expensive or unavailable."

Investigative business journalist Gary Weiss, who now writes for *Portfolio*, exposed nefarious behavior on Wall Street in his 2007 book, "Wall Street Versus America: A Muckraking Look at the Thieves, Fakers and Charlatans Who Are Ripping You Off." The title pretty much sums it up.

[A]nybody who's been paying attention has seen business journalists waving the red flag for several years.

They Reported That Trouble Was Brewing

Although business news coverage often struggles to explain the complexities of the field to average citizens, writers such as Morgenson and Pearlstein avoid the jargon found elsewhere. They made it clear that serious trouble was brewing in the economy and on Wall Street.

Here's the issue that financial journalism faces: No one likes a nattering nabob of negativism, especially when the stock market is climbing and all of our 401(k) plans are tied to it. So we shut out what we don't want to hear because it conflicts with what we'd like to happen.

To be sure, the business media haven't been perfect. Both *Fortune* and *Forbes*, for example, sang the praises of Merrill Lynch CEO John Thain in 2008, shortly before the company was forced to sell itself to Bank of America or risk going under. Forbes went so far as to say the financial house was in "damn good shape." And the personal finance magazines that tout the best stocks and mutual funds can be maddening because they rarely, if ever, outperform the market. Do they really think they—or the so-called experts they're interviewing—know?

But anybody who's been paying attention has seen business journalists waving the red flag for several years. "The fact that housing was a bubble was printed millions of times," says Allan Sloan, a *Fortune* columnist and arguably the country's preeminent business journalist. "This is one time that we did what we were supposed to do."

The powerful players in business journalism include the Wall Street Journal, *the business sections of the* New York Times *and the* Washington Post.

Don't just take the business journalists' word for it. Their effectiveness in naming the scoundrels is supported by academic research. In 2003, then-Harvard Business School professor Greg Miller studied more than 260 cases of accounting fraud. He determined that nearly a third of them were identified by the business media before the Securities and Exchange Commission [SEC] or the company said they were targets of investigations. "In each of these articles, it is the reporter making the case for accounting impropriety based on analysis of public and private information," wrote Miller, who now teaches at the University of Michigan. "No other information intermediaries (i.e. analysts, auditors, or the legal system) are cited."

In other words, business journalists, who have no regulatory power over the companies and the economy, have been proactive in their coverage.

The current economic crisis and Wall Street turmoil have been caused by developments in the housing market. Lenders, in a bid to continue growing, extended credit to homebuyers who previously might not have qualified for a loan. They then sold many of those dubious loans to investors to get them off their books, allowing the lenders to make yet more questionable loans. The packages of loans purchased by the investors are called credit derivatives. The investors thought they were buying loans that had been properly vetted—but they hadn't been.

Buyers Were Not Aware

Meanwhile, many homebuyers were unaware of the terms of the contracts they were signing. Others were speculating in the real estate market, purchasing homes they simply wanted to flip to another buyer for a higher price.

A market based on rickety credit, fraud and speculation can grow for only so long. Regulators from the Federal Reserve Board to the SEC kept it going for as long as possible by relaxing some of their regulations on lending and debt. When real estate prices started to fall in the spring and summer of 2007, loans that had been sold to investors began to sour, and derivatives that lenders such as Fannie Mae had purchased as investments to protect themselves against higher interest rates led to more risk on their balance sheets than they could handle. These derivatives were no longer worth their purchase price because of the decline in the value of the real estate that backed them.

That created the current unpleasantness, with the federal government pumping $700 billion into the economy and billions more into endangered companies to avert another depression like the massive one of the 1930s.

The powerful players in business journalism include the *Wall Street Journal*, the business sections of the *New York Times* and the *Washington Post*, and business magazines such as *BusinessWeek* and *Fortune*. These are the news outlets with the power to direct the conversation. Readers who care about business and the economy—from investors to regulators to company executives—read these publications.

An examination of their work before spring 2007, when the first cracks began to appear in housing and investments, reveals ample coverage of the dangers that lay ahead.

And it wasn't just the business media elite. A number of smaller news organizations distinguished themselves by spotlighting the rampant problems. The *Charlotte Observer*, for example, ran a series in March 2007 about an unscrupulous homebuilding firm that caused the company to stop making loans and leave the area. In fact, 11 winners in the most recent Society of American Business Editors and Writers' Best in Business contest—for material published in 2007—focused on the mortgage mess or credit problems. Regional and metro papers, for the most part, covered the housing and credit issues well, but did so from a local angle and didn't convey the broad perspective that the national business media provided.

Let's start with the *Wall Street Journal*, considered the top business newspaper in the country, if not the world. Marcus Brauchli, now executive editor of the *Washington Post*, returned to the United States at the end of 1999 after reporting from China to become the *Journal's* national editor. He immediately took an interest in the *Journal's* coverage, then overseen by Constance Mitchell-Ford, of government-backed housing lenders Fannie Mae and Freddie Mac, two of the largest lenders in the country. The first page-one story questioning the lenders' practices ran on July 14, 2000. Brauchli was called to Fannie Mae's headquarters in 2001 to meet with CEO Franklin Raines, who was upset about the tone of the articles. "He felt we were unduly critical," Brauchli remembers. "We were just reporting the facts."

Excesses Were Revealed

The *Journal* published numerous stories about the lenders, hammering away at the excesses it uncovered—often on the front page. On January 2, 2002, reporters Jathon Sapsford and Patrick Barta wrote about the dramatic increase in consumer lending. On August 6 of that year, Barta followed up with a 2,400-word examination of Fannie and Freddie that asked, "With homeownership already so high, are Fannie and Freddie running out of room to grow?" In the fifth paragraph, he wrote, "The huge size and rapid growth, coupled with their concentration in a single industry, has brought concern about possible risk to the U.S. economy should one of them ever fail."

A month later, on September 17, a Barta story on the front of the *Journal's* Money & Investing section pointed out the increased risk on Fannie's financial statements because of falling interest rates. On August 19, 2003, Barta and fellow reporter Ruth Simon wrote a front-page story on the hidden closing costs for mortgages.

Nikhil Deogun, a former editor of the Journal's Money & Investing *section and now deputy managing editor, says the coverage was intentionally repetitive to hammer home the point.*

And a month later, a 3,000-word bombshell on Freddie, written by Barta, John D. McKinnon and Gregory Zuckerman, appeared on the *Journal's* front page. They wrote: "Far from the sleepy mortgage company of its carefully cultivated reputation, Freddie Mac in recent years has evolved into a giant, sophisticated investment company, running a business laden with volatility and complexity. That change has sent risks soaring, not just for investors but for U.S. taxpayers, who likely would be on the hook if the federally chartered company stumbled."

Stories about the increasing uncertainty in the real estate market appeared regularly in the *Journal* for the next several years until the market imploded. A May 2005 front-page story focused on homeowners who took on too much debt while buying real estate. An August 2005 front-page story examined the fact that lenders were selling more mortgages because investors wanted the securities that backed them. James Hagerty wrote a front-page story on March 11, 2006, about the dangers of adjustable-rate mortgages. In December 2006, a front-page article about the increase of delinquent subprime mortgages appeared, noting, "If late payments and foreclosures continue to rise at a faster-than-expected pace, the pain could extend beyond homeowners and lenders to the investors who buy mortgage-backed securities."

Another *Journal* reporter, Jesse Eisinger, wrote extensively during this period about the risks posed by derivatives. And since joining *Portfolio* in 2006, Eisinger has repeatedly written about how derivatives might cause turmoil on Wall Street, going as far as to predict in a November 2007 cover story that Bear Stearns and Lehman Brothers would struggle to remain independent.

Nikhil Deogun, a former editor of the *Journal*'s Money & Investing section and now deputy managing editor, says the coverage was intentionally repetitive to hammer home the point. "People may not have heard you, so you have to explore different angles to tell the same story a different way," he says. "I'm kind of curious as to why is it that people were shocked, given the volume of coverage."

Hammering Home the Point

Meanwhile, the *New York Times* and the *Washington Post* were sounding warnings of their own. In the *Times* on October 3, 2004, in a story headlined "A Coming Nightmare of Homeownership?" Morgenson wrote, "The most damaging legacy of Fannie Mae's years of unchecked growth may not be evident until the next significant economic slump." Alongside Morgenson's story that day was another on Fannie Mae, by Timothy L. O'Brien and Jennifer B. Lee, that said, "If the company encounters serious setbacks, the impact on homeowners and the world's financial markets could be unpleasant."

When she wasn't writing about housing, Morgenson was detailing the continued excesses of executive compensation and the credit markets.

The *Times*' Henriques wrote a series of articles exposing instant lenders who preyed on military households, pushing high-cost loans with interest rates much higher than the norm. Unlike many other pieces, her reporting set off a firestorm. Congress held hearings on the practice and passed laws to ban it.

Henriques believes she knows why regulators paid attention to her stories but ignored others about lending practices that were far worse because they were hurting investment portfolios. A friend who works for a big institutional investor was called to Washington, D.C., to speak to lawmakers before the first vote on the [George W.] Bush administration's bailout plan in September [2008]. The friend noticed that all of the televisions in Congressional offices were tuned to coverage of Capitol Hill on C-SPAN, not to CNBC or Fox Business Network. "He said nothing had struck him so powerfully about how lawmakers had been cut off from what was happening on Wall Street," Henriques says. "As a business journalist, we were talking to a glass window. They were sealed off from what we were writing."

Also exploring the dangers on the horizon was the *Times*' Floyd Norris, whose coverage of creative accounting during this period was prescient. Time after time, he wrote about how companies, including Fannie Mae, were pushing regulators to relax standards and stretch the rules as far as they could, just a few years after Enron's manipulation of accounting regulations helped push the company into bankruptcy court.

The *Post's* Pearlstein also shed light on the economy's pitfalls. At least someone noticed his work: Pearlstein won a 2008 Pulitzer Prize in commentary—the first ever given to a business columnist—for a series of columns about the impending economic turmoil.

Burrowing into a Dangerous Landscape

These reporters weren't alone. Their colleagues at business magazines burrowed into the dangerous financial landscape and unearthed alarming stories as well.

Shawn Tully at *Fortune* raised serious questions about the housing market as far back as October 2002, when he wrote, "U.S. housing prices are stretching the outer limits of what's reasonable and sustainable. Instead of cooling down, prices keep hurtling upward, defying the laws of economic gravity just as grievously as those unmentionable dot-coms once did."

In September 2004, Tully was back with a big story. The headline blared, "Is the Housing Boom Over? Home prices have gone up for so long that people think they'll never come down. But the fundamentals tell a different story—a scary one." And in July 2005, Tully offered advice for how people near retirement could get the most from selling their houses in the "overheated real estate market." In May 2006, Tully wrote about the beginning of the decline of the housing market.

Not to be outdone, *Fortune's* Bethany McLean—one of the first to expose Enron's problems—wrote two stories highly critical of Fannie Mae in early 2005. And then there's Loomis' prophetic 1994 story about derivatives—the magazine trotted it out in mid-2008 and posted it on its home page.

At *BusinessWeek,* banking and finance editor Mara Der Hovanesian chipped away as well. Her September 11, 2006, cover story, "Nightmare Mortgages," was illustrated by a snake slowly squeezing the life out of a home. It covered everything from deceptive loan practices to investors willing to buy risky loan portfolios. The previous year, Der Hovanesian wrote about derivatives, essentially warning about a pending credit meltdown. "Surprises similar to Enron and WorldCom—large, investment-grade companies that fall from grace overnight—could roil markets," she wrote in a May 2005 story.

Her colleagues hit Wall Street equally hard. An April 2006 piece titled "Mortgage Lenders: Who's Most at Risk" exposed the subprime lending problems likely to face many finance companies. A June 2006 *BusinessWeek* cover story raised warnings about Wall Street's enthusiastic embrace of risk. And the magazine regularly published shorter stories about potential economic problems on the horizon.

"We were aggressive. We were aware. We wrote abundantly. But it is very hard to get the public's attention for stories warning of complex financial risks in the middle of a roaring, populist bull market."

Why the Surprise?

So if business journalists did such a good job sounding the alarm about the nation's economic house of cards, why did its collapse seem to come as such a shock? Why wasn't anyone listening?

Andrew Leckey, director of the Donald W. Reynolds National Center for Business Journalism at Arizona State University, compares the situation to an unwanted Christmas present wrapped in shiny paper and a bow: Nobody wants to open it up to see what's inside. The reading public wants to read only what it wants to believe. Brauchli agrees: "The notion that the business press wasn't paying attention is wrong, and the assertion that we were asleep at the switch is wrong. We were attentive. We were aggressive. We were aware. We wrote abundantly. But it is very hard to get the public's attention for stories warning of complex financial risks in the middle of a roaring, populist bull market."

Leckey believes that one way to get readers to pay more attention would be for regulators to require greater transparency regarding the quality of loans that lenders are making and that investors are purchasing. That will allow business journalists to more fully investigate the loan market and inform readers of the true creditworthiness of homebuyers. He believes that will give stories the power they need to resonate with readers. "It wasn't loud enough to alter anyone's behavior," Leckey says. "The information was out there, but I don't think we knew the level of the subprime that some of these companies like Merrill Lynch had on their books."

"People don't want to read it. The culture encouraged people to minimize risk. Nobody wanted to think about risk. We don't celebrate thrift in this country."

Henriques, who grades the print business media from B+ to A in the run-up to today's crisis, agrees with Leckey, adding that business journalists can do one thing to raise the volume of their alarms: Connect more clearly the dots between Washington policy, or the lack thereof, and events on Wall Street. "To some extent, there will be lessons on both sides," Henriques says. "On our side will be that business journalists will have to expand the notion of whom we're writing for and more clearly enunciate the policy decisions."

But Brauchli worries about journalists becoming overly negative in the wake of the subprime lending schedule. "You can't scaremonger," he says. "I'm not suggesting for a moment that journalists shouldn't be aggressive. But journalists, like markets, tend to overshoot. You don't want to go overboard and celebrate the downturn."

Bartlett, the former business journalist who now teaches at CUNY [City University of New York], argues that the media could be at the forefront of educating readers on personal finance topics such as the value of long-term saving instead of promoting how to acquire more money as fast as possible. But, she says, "People don't want to read it. The culture encouraged people to minimize risk. Nobody wanted to think about risk. We don't celebrate thrift in this country."

Deogun, the *Wall Street Journal* deputy managing editor, agrees with Bartlett about the need to better educate readers, noting the growing complexity of financial products such as adjustable-rate mortgages. "There is a tendency sometimes to get really caught up, particularly in personal finance journalism, to write about the latest product that a bank is selling," he says. "These are products. They're no different than Coca-Cola producing a new drink, or PepsiCo coming out with a new line of potato chips. It doesn't mean that it's good for the consumer."

Deogun believes that some readers now understand that business journalists can give them the information they need. He points to the *Journal's* September newsstand sales, which spiked 20 percent. "We're selling out now," he says. "There's clearly a desire from readers to know what's going on and to navigate their way through [the crisis]. Where were they earlier?"

12

Bias Often Distorts the Reporting of Science News

Charles W. Schmidt

Charles W. Schmidt has written for Discover *magazine,* Science, *and* Nature Medicine. *He is a 2002 winner of the National Association of Science Writers' Science-in-Society Journalism Award.*

An article in the June 2009 issue of Nature Biotechnology *argued that since the advent of the World Wide Web, media fragmentation and the rise of intensely ideological websites has contributed to increasing polarization of public opinion around some scientific issues. Individuals tend to migrate toward news sources that reinforce opinions they already hold. Given the ease with which bias can shape public perceptions about research and technology, and given the importance of contemporary debates over climate change, health, and energy, scientists need to think carefully about the way they communicate with the public.*

Mojib Latif probably didn't anticipate the public reaction his research would attract. . . . Writing in the May 2008 issue of *Nature*, he and his colleagues from the Leibniz Institute of Marine Sciences and the Max Planck Institute in Kiel, Germany, predicted that increases in mean global temperatures could pause into the next decade, even though greenhouse gas levels were still rising in the atmosphere. That lull in warming, their models showed, was temporary, and due to complex interactions between the atmosphere and periodic cooling cycles in the oceans.

Charles W. Schmidt, "Communication Gap: The Disconnect Between What Scientists Say and What the Public Hears," *Environmental Health Perspectives*, vol. 117, no. 12, December 2009. Reproduced with Permission from *Environmental Health Perspectives*.

A meteorologist and oceanographer, Latif emphasized that these cyclical variations could occur even in the face of long-term climate trends. But to his surprise, skeptics seized on the findings as evidence that mean global temperatures aren't really rising. The website newsbusters.org, for instance, which bills itself as "dedicated to documenting, exposing, and neutralizing liberal media bias," compared Latif's findings to "the Pope suddenly [announcing] the Catholic Church had been wrong for centuries about prohibiting priests from marrying." To Latif, the implication that climate change is a hoax was preposterous. "Making inferences about global warming from my short-term climate prediction is like comparing apples and oranges," he says.

Latif was caught in a familiar media trap. Research often delivers statistically nuanced findings that the lay public as well as journalists and other science communicators can find hard to understand. And just as political messages can be twisted into snippets of misinformation, scientific findings, too, are vulnerable to distortions and misrepresentations that stick in the public mind, especially if they fit ideologic biases.

Scientists need to somehow communicate scientific uncertainties while going head-to-head against oversimplified inaccuracies in the media. The question is how best to do that.

Gridlocked Opinions

These distortions are becoming all too common in today's new media environment. Although the World Wide Web offers invaluable access to information, it also gives an audience to anyone with an ax to grind. According to a commentary in the June 2009 issue of *Nature Biotechnology* authored by 24 experts in communication, law, and journalism, media fragmentation and the rise of ideologically slanted websites are perpetuating gridlocked opinions in science, just as they are in politics.

One of those authors is Matthew Nisbet, an assistant professor of communication at American University in Washington, DC. He says people who aren't inclined to pay close attention to an issue will learn about it from media outlets that reinforce their own social, political, or religious views. This and other types of "mental shortcuts," he says, make it possible for individuals to draw quick conclusions about complex topics that fit their own preconceptions.

Given these trends, communication experts are calling for fundamental changes in how scientists interact with the media because debates over climate change, health, energy, and technology are simply too important to lose to misinformation. As always, scientists are encouraged to communicate clearly using language that nonspecialists can understand. But now they're also being urged to step beyond the confines of the laboratory and to become more engaged in efforts to educate the public.

"The ultimate goal [in science communication]," says Nisbet, "is civic education—enabling and motivating more people into thinking, talking, and participating in collective decisions about, for example, what to do about climate change, or how to fund and oversee biotechnology." Scientists need to somehow communicate scientific uncertainties while going head-to-head against oversimplified inaccuracies in the media. The question is how best to do that.

Reworking the Angle

Nisbet in particular seeks to move beyond the traditional "deficit model" that currently dominates science communication. The deficit model assumes that if nonspecialists only understood the scientific facts, they would see eye-to-eye with the experts. Ignorance is what drives controversies in science, the model postulates. And by filling that deficit with knowledge, scientists can help make these controversies disappear.

But does that assumption really hold true? Not necessarily, Nisbet says. Disputes over climate change, for instance, remain strong despite the sustained efforts of scientists to communicate about the issue through the media. An October 2009 survey by the Pew Research Center for the People & the Press suggests public opinions about climate change line up more on political than scientific grounds.

According to that survey, 75% of Democrats see solid evidence that the average temperature on Earth has been getting warmer over the past few decades, compared with just 35% of Republicans. That disparity, Nisbet says, reflects opposing media influences geared toward their respective audiences. Both Republicans and Democrats tend to rely on news outlets that affirm their own social values, he says. And those outlets—together with input from like-minded friends and colleagues—can be more influential than the science itself.

Tellingly, the Pew survey also indicates that, compared with survey responses from April 2008, 8% fewer Democrats and 14% fewer Republicans reported seeing solid evidence of warming, which suggests confidence in the research is declining across party lines. The surveyors do not comment, however, on the reasons for that decline or whether it might reflect contradictory coverage of climate change in the press.

Telling Personally Relevant Stories

Nisbet is well known for his research on framing, or defining scientific issues in ways that audiences can understand in part by appealing to their core values. Climate change skeptics already do this successfully by predicting economic doom from curbing greenhouse gas emissions, he says. "You need to use metaphors and narratives that make the issue personally relevant," Nisbet explains. "It's got to be understandable and interesting to audiences that don't understand the technical details."

Teaming with evangelical leaders has enabled some scientists to frame climate change in terms of religious morality, which helps to engage conservative Christians on the issue. Among them are Eric Chivian, director of the Center for Health and the Global Environment at the Harvard Medical School, and Richard Cizik, founder and president of the recently formed New Evangelicals, who famously joined forces in 2007 to educate law makers and the public about environmental threats. Cizik is quoted in the 18 November 2009 online edition of the U.K. *Guardian* as saying that younger generations of evangelicals in particular "have an intensity level that even some in the environmental community don't have. They believe [environmental stewardship] is their God-given calling."

But Sharon Dunwoody, a professor of journalism and mass communication at the University of Wisconsin-Madison, cautious that frames might be labeled as spin by audiences who feel they're being manipulated. A climate change activist, for instance, might think it's effective to frame climate change in terms of dying polar bears. But a skeptic who doesn't think polar bears are at risk from climate change might feel manipulated by that frame and view it as spin.

To that, Nisbet says, "'Spin' is a problematic term since people use it in multiple ways and really never define what they mean by it. They usually just throw it out there as a way to express criticism without actually explaining what their criticism might be, or what their preferred alternative is."

Maintaining Credibility

Framing can pose other tough challenges for scientists; it requires them to know and understand what elements will engage a given target audience. And that begs insights into human nature that might not come readily to those more comfortable with data. Nisbet says talking points for use in framing can be obtained from research techniques familiar to social sciences research, such as interviews, focus groups, and surveys. Results from these investigations can be translated into practical advice for scientists who interact with different audiences via media formats such as web and video, he says.

Holland's view is that university news offices and what he describes as "support networks for the scientific community" bear responsibility for couching how research findings enter into policy debates—not the scientists themselves.

Earl Holland, assistant vice president for research communications at The Ohio State University, argues that scientists are preoccupied with the day-to-day grinds of publishing and research, and therefore shouldn't be obliged to consider public perceptions of their work so explicitly. He suggests, moreover, that those activities might compromise a scientist's integrity.

Scientists often have the trust of the public going for them—they're typically held in high esteem, Holland says. What elevates scientists over those who spread misinformation, he explains, is credibility, and that credibility lies in part on the notion that scientists make impartial judgments based on data. But when they align themselves with a particular side in a debate, that impartiality is put to the test, he says.

Some Believe Advocacy Damages Credibility

"As soon as scientists take up an advocacy role, regardless of the position or topic, they lose credibility as unbiased sources," Holland asserts. "Some say that's too much to ask, but I say that just like journalists have to rein in their own political beliefs when reporting, scientists have to avoid catering to policy arguments. They're still highly regarded, but if they just get in there and punch it out with their opponents, they risk losing integrity."

Holland's view is that university news offices and what he describes as "support networks for the scientific community" bear responsibility for couching how research findings enter into policy debates—not the scientists themselves. That's not a universal view, however; many scientists see no problem with advocacy, as long as it's guided by expertise and experience.

Bruce Lanphear, a professor at BC Children's Hospital and Simon Fraser University in Vancouver, British Columbia, says debates over whether scientists should get involved in policy are mostly semantic. "There's a certain school of thought that our job as epidemiologists is simply to report results in journals while others translate those findings for the public—I don't subscribe to that," he says. "I view my job as also helping to translate findings in ways that don't mislead the public but that also help people understand why something is important."

Lanphear is best known for research that links low-dose exposure to lead and other toxicants to developmental effects in children. As a medical doctor, he says his efforts to raise awareness about industrial toxicants in commerce are consistent with the Hippocratic Oath. "Activism is a direct extension of what I was trained to do as a doctor," he says. "I feel an obligation to present data in ways that prevent dangerous exposures in the population."

Lanphear appears unfazed by charges of alarmism, and he acknowledges there remain many unanswered toxilogic questions about lead, pesticides, and other chemicals. But their known risks also compel regulatory changes to minimize exposure, he says. In communicating about low-dose chemical risks, Lanphear aims to create a sense of urgency, which he says is a prerequisite to environmental legislation.

"That's what it comes down to: community outrage," Lan-phear says. "We knew lead was toxic as far back as 1909. Why did it take so long to restrict how we use it? Because of iner-tia, lobbyists, and the tax revenues it was generating. It took outrage and lawsuits to move the legislation. A sense of ur-gency holds feet to the fire."

Aiming for Clarity

People might look to science for clear-cut statements that can help them make decisions about their health and lifestyle, says Louis Guillette, Jr., a professor of biology at the University of Florida at Gainesville. But fields such as climate research, ge-nomics, and toxicology are all grappling with enormous data sets and models that generate probabilistic instead of defini-tive findings. Most genetic tests, for instance, can't accurately predict if someone will get a disease; they can only suggest that someone has perhaps a 15% chance of getting the disease under certain environmental conditions. Likewise, climate models can simulate temperature changes, but they can't pre-dict exactly where or when impacts will occur.

Individuals looking for clarity with respect to environ-mental threats might want a scientist to say, for instance, that a chemical will cause a specific effect at a precise real-world dose, but laboratory experiments don't allow for that, adds Guillette. Instead, experiments deliberately exclude confound-ing factors such as age, sex, or hormonal status to isolate a single variable's effect on a particular outcome. In the real world, these variables work simultaneously, along with a host of other chemical exposures, to produce effects that vary by individual.

It's important to provide the public with a baseline con-text for understanding what's meant by "risk," experts say. For instance, it's meaningless to say that family history of a disease makes a person 10 times more likely to succumb to that dis-ease. It is clearer to say that if 1 in 100,000 people in the general population has the disease, then family history increases the risk to 1 in 10,000. That still may be a noteworthy difference—but perhaps not cause for undue alarm.

It's also important to specify what groups are being compared when talking about changes in risk so it's clear whether those changes are being described in absolute or relative terms. For example, consider preeclampsia, which effects an estimated 4% of pregnancies. If an environmental exposure increases the absolute risk of preeclampsia by 30%, that would mean going from 4% to 34%. In contrast, a relative increase of 30% would mean going from 4% to 5.2%.

All these statistical details make it impossible for scientists to speak in absolutes, so they communicate instead in terms of statistical probabilities that ideally apply under most real-world scenarios. Scientists take these nuances for granted, but they make a world of difference to anyone who has to interpret what new findings mean on a practical level. That's an essential issue, because research must somehow reconcile data with society's desire for clarity on scientific issues.

Joann Rodgers, senior advisor for science, crisis, and executive communications at Johns Hopkins Medicine and past president of the National Association of Science Writers, says environmental health findings are particularly hard to convey because, in addition to their complexity, they evoke emotional responses; climate change, pollution, and many other environmental threats affect millions of people. "Environmental issues give rise to a lot of activism," Rodgers says. "We tend to see that also in other fields, but there seems to be an extraordinary dose of mythologizing and ranting about science in the environmental health realm."

Dunwoody emphasizes that, as sources in the media, scientists get to decide what they're going to say. But she adds they should also be insightful about how those messages are received, given the need to dispel misinformation in the public arena. "The way you portray something dictates the take-home messages people walk away with," she says. "You've got to be careful."

Organizations to Contact

The editors have compiled the following list of organizations concerned with the issues debated in this book. The descriptions are derived from materials provided by the organizations. All have publications or information available for interested readers. The list was compiled on the date of publication of the present volume; the information provided here may change. Be aware that many organizations take several weeks or longer to respond to inquiries, so allow as much time as possible.

Accuracy in Media (AIM)
4455 Connecticut Avenue, N.W., Suite 330
Washington, DC   20008
(202) 364-4401 • fax: (202) 364-4098
e-mail: info@aim.org
website: www.aim.org

Accuracy in Media is a citizens' media organization whose mission is to promote accuracy, fairness, and balance in news reporting. AIM exposes politically motivated media bias, teaches consumers to think critically about their news sources, and holds the mainstream press accountable for its misreporting. Columns, reports, blogs, briefings, and podcasts are available at its website.

American Society of News Editors (ASNE)
11690B Sunrise Valley Dr., Reston, VA   20191-1409
(703) 453-1122 • fax: (703) 453-1133
website: http://asne.org

The American Society of News Editors is a nonprofit professional organization that focuses on leadership development and journalism-related issues. ASNE promotes fair, principled journalism, defends and protects First Amendment rights, and fights for freedom of information and open government.

Other key initiatives include leadership, innovation, diversity and inclusion in coverage and the journalism work force, youth journalism, and the sharing of ideas. ASNE produces such webinars as *Enterprise and Watchdog Reporting in Smaller News Organizations.*

Association of Health Care Journalists (AHCJ)
Missouri School of Journalism, 10 Neff Hall
Columbia, MO 65211
(573) 884-5606 • fax: (573) 884-5609
e-mail: info@healthjournalism.org
website: www.healthjournalism.org

The Association of Health Care Journalists is a nonprofit organization dedicated to advancing public understanding of health care issues by improving the quality, accuracy, and visibility of health care reporting, writing, and editing. AHCJ publishes a quarterly newsletter, *Healthbeat,* and several guides to covering specific aspects of health and health care, including *Covering Obesity: A Guide for Reporters.*

The Authentic Voice: The Best Reporting on Race and Ethnicity
Arlene Morgan, Associate Dean, Columbia University
Graduate School of Journalism, 2950 Broadway MC 3800
New York, NY 10027
e-mail: am494@columbia.edu
website: www.theauthenticvoice.org

The Authentic Voice: The Best Reporting on Race and Ethnicity is a multimedia teaching tool that includes a book, DVD, and a website. The project is based on a collection of award-winning stories from the Let's Do It Better! Workshop on Journalism, Race and Ethnicity at the Columbia University Graduate School of Journalism. Ted Koppel, former anchor of *Nightline,* Bob Simon of *60 Minutes, New York Times* reporter Mirta Ojito, and Anne Hull of the *Washington Post* are among the contributors. They discuss challenges, mistakes, ethical issues, and the work that goes into quality reporting when a story involves race and/or ethnicity.

The Center for Public Integrity

910 17th Street NW, Suite 700, Washington, DC   20006
(202) 466-1300
website: www.publicintegrity.org

The mission of the Center for Public Integrity is to produce original investigative journalism about morally significant public issues, in order to make institutional power more transparent and accountable. The Center's investigative reports, articles, and blogs are available at its website, as well as an e-mail newsletter.

Media Research Center (MRC)

325 S. Patrick Street, Alexandria, VA   22314
(703) 683-9733 • fax: (703) 683-9736
website: www.mrc.org/public/default.aspx

Leaders of America's conservative movement have long believed that within the national news media a strident liberal bias existed that influenced the public's understanding of critical issues. The mission of the Media Research Center is to bring balance to the news media, and it coordinates a comprehensive media monitoring operation. The MRC's publications include annual reports, Bias Alerts, Media Reality Check Reports, and columns by founder L. Brent Bozell.

The National Press Club (NPC)

529 14th Street, NW, 13th Floor, Washington, DC   20045
(202) 662-7500
website: http://press.org

The National Press Club, based in Washington, DC, was founded in 1908 to promote free press and provide benefits to journalists. With a membership that includes writers, editors, authors, reporters, producers, journalism professors, and students, it is an advocate for the press around the nation and around the world. Radio Broadcasts from the Club, programs featuring NPC luncheon speakers, and original roundtable discussions, are available at NPC's website.

The Newseum

555 Pennsylvania Ave. N.W., Washington, DC   20001

(888) 639-7386

website: www.newseum.org

The Newseum, located in Washington, DC, is a 250,000-square-foot museum of news that documents five centuries of news history, using contemporary technology and hands-on exhibits. Its mission is to educate the public about the value of a free press in a free society. The main funder of the Newseum is the Freedom Forum, a nonpartisan foundation that champions the First Amendment as a cornerstone of democracy. The Newseum website includes resources for teachers and students.

Pew Research Center's Project for Excellence in Journalism (PEJ)

1615 L Street N.W., Suite 700, Washington, DC   20036

(202) 419-3650

e-mail: mail@journalism.org

website: www.journalism.org

The Pew Research Center's Project for Excellence in Journalism (PEJ) specializes in using empirical methods to evaluate and study the performance of the press, particularly content analysis. Its goal is to help both the journalists who produce the news and the citizens who consume it develop a better understanding of what the press is delivering, how the media are changing, and what forces are shaping those changes. Each year PEJ publishes a report, *The State of the News Media*, on current issues and challenges shaping American journalism. The website also includes *Who Owns the News Media*, an interactive database of companies that own news properties in the United States.

ProPublica

One Exchange Plaza, 55 Broadway, 23rd Floor
New York, NY 10006
(212) 514-5250 • fax: (212) 785-2634
website: www.propublica.org

ProPublica was created as a response to the business crisis in publishing, which has made in-depth investigative reporting increasingly unaffordable for many news organizations. It is an independent, non-profit newsroom that produces investigative journalism in the public interest. Reports such as "Eye on Loan Modifications" and "Buried Secrets: Gas Drilling's Environmental Threat," along with news applications, graphics, databases, and tools, can be found on its website.

Radio Television Digital News Association (RTDNA)

RTDNA/RTDNF, 4121 Plank Rd., #512
Fredericksburg, VA 22407
(202) 659-6510 • fax: (202) 223-4007
website: www.rtnda.org

RTDNA is the world's largest professional organization exclusively serving the electronic news profession. The Radio Television Digital News Foundation, the educational arm of the association, was created to help RTDNF members embody and uphold the standards of ethical journalism and promote leadership in the newsroom. The website includes a Best Practices page that addresses ethical issues in newsgathering and reporting.

Society of Professional Journalists (SPJ)

Eugene S. Pulliam National Journalism Center
3909 N. Meridian St., Indianapolis, IN 46208
(317) 927-8000 • fax: (317) 920-4789
website: http://spj.org

SPJ is a professional organization that includes broadcast, print and online journalists, educators, and students. The mission of SPJ includes the following: to promote the flow of information, to protect First Amendment guarantees of freedom of speech and of the press, to stimulate high standards and ethical behavior in the practice of journalism, to foster excellence among journalists, and to encourage a climate in which journalism can be practiced freely. Resources for journalists, such as blogs, articles, and guidelines on ethics and diversity, are available at its website.

Bibliography

Books

Stuart Allan — *The Routledge Companion to News and Journalism*. London: Routledge, 2010.

Geofffrey Baym — *From Cronkite to Colbert: The Evolution of Broadcast News*. Boulder: Paradigm Publishers, 2010.

Larry Beinhart — *Fog Facts: Searching for Truth in the Land of Spin*. New York: Nation Books, 2005.

W. Joseph Campbell — *Getting It Wrong: Ten of the Greatest Misreported Stories in American Journalism*. Berkeley: University of California Press, 2010.

David Craig — *The Ethics of the Story: Using Narrative Techniques Responsibly in Journalism*. Lanham: Rowman & Littlefield, 2006.

Ken Doctor — *Newsonomics: Twelve New Trends That Will Shape the News You Get*. New York: St. Martin's Press, 2010.

David Edwards and David Cromwell — *Newspeak in the 21st Century*. London: Pluto, 2009.

Erika Falk — *Women for President: Media Bias in Nine Campaigns*. Urbana: University of Illinois Press, 2010.

Jack Fuller

What Is Happening to News: The Information Explosion and the Crisis in Journalism. Chicago: University of Chicago Press, 2010.

Howard Good and Sandra L. Bendon

Ethics and Entertainment: Essays on Media Culture and Media Morality. Jefferson, NC: McFarland & Company, Inc., 2010.

Amy Goodman and David Goodman

Static: Government Liars, Media Cheerleaders and the People Who Fight Back. New York: Hyperion, 2006.

Neil Henry

American Carnival: Journalism Under Siege in an Age of New Media. Berkeley: University of California Press, 2007.

Ralph S. Izard and Jay Perkins

Covering Disaster: Lessons from Media Coverage of Katrina and Rita. New Brunswick, NJ: Transaction Publishers, 2010.

Alex S. Jones

Losing the News: The Future of the News That Feeds Democracy. New York: Oxford University Press, 2009.

Dave Kindred

Morning Miracle: Inside the Washington Post; A Great Newspaper Fights for Its Life. New York: Doubleday, 2010.

Bill Kovach and Tom Rosenstiel

The Elements of Journalism: What Newspeople Should Know and the Public Should Expect. New York: Three Rivers Press, 2007.

Laurel Leff — *Buried by the Times: The Holocaust and America's Most Important Newspaper*. New York: Cambridge University Press, 2005.

Farhad Manjoo — *True Enough: Learning to Live in a Post-Fact Society*. Hoboken: Wiley, 2008.

Robert Waterman McChesney and John Nichols — *The Death and Life of American Journalism: The Media Revolution That Will Begin the World Again*. Philadelphia: Nation Books, 2010.

Philip Meyer — *Newspaper Ethics in the New Century: A Report to the American Society of Newspaper Editors*. Reston, VA: American Society of Newspaper Editors, 2006.

Bill D. Moyers — *Moyers on Democracy*. New York: Doubleday, 2008.

John Nichols and Robert Waterman McChesney — *Tragedy and Farce: How the American Media Sell Wars, Spin Elections and Destroy Democracy*. New York: New Press, 2005.

Nicholas J. Russell — *Communicating Science: Professional, Popular, Literary*. New York: Cambridge University Press, 2010.

Paul Starr — *The Creation of the Media: Political Origins of Modern Communications*. New York: Basic Books, 2004.

Mike Wallace and Beth Knobel — *Heat and Light: Advice for the Next Generation of Journalists*. New York: Three Rivers Press, 2010.

Lee Wilkins and Renita Coleman — *The Moral Media: How Journalists Reason About Ethics.* Mahwah, NJ: Lawrence Erlbaum Associates, 2005.

Jim Willis — *The Mind of a Journalist: How Reporters View Themselves, Their World, and Their Craft.* Los Angeles: Sage, 2010.

Periodicals

Philip Bell — "Measuring Bias? It's Not as Easy ABC," *The Age*, October 26, 2006.

Eric Boehlert — "Andrew Breitbart's Mainstream Demise," *MediaMatters for America*, November 3, 2010.

Kamna Bohra — "Media Bias Degrades Legitimate Content," *Technique* (Georgia Tech University), November 5, 2010.

Kevin Drum — "Narrative Woes," *Washington Monthly*, May 19, 2009.

Jeffrey A. Dvorkin — "Is Liberal Bias What NPR Listeners Secretly Want?" *NPR*, June 28, 2005.

Eve Fairbanks — "Embrace Your Media Bias," *Politics Magazine*, November 2008.

Conor Friedersdorf — "Electric Kool-Aid Conservatism," *Doublethink Online*, May 19, 2008.

Jonah Goldberg — "The New Frontier: 'Covering' Conservatives," *USA Today*, July 6, 2010.

Jennifer Harper   "Majority, in All Political Camps, Cite News Bias," *Washington Times* March 2, 2010.

Kevin A. Hassett   "Who Is Really on the March?" *National Review*, November 15, 2010.

Investor's Business Daily   "Media Bias: The Chasm Widens," September 10, 2010.

Jeff Jarvis   "Objectivity Is a Lie, So the Truth Requires Real Citizen Journalism," *Guardian UK*, November 1, 2010.

William S. Jasper   "Media Bias," *New American*, May 24, 2010.

Michelle T. Johnson   "Why Bias Shows Up in Surprising Places," *Kansas City Star*, November 1, 2010.

Patrik Jonsson   "Shirley Sherrod: Does She Have a Case Against Andrew Breitbart?" *Christian Science Monitor*, July 29, 2010.

Garry Leech   "The Need for Journalistic Bias," *Columbia Reports*, October 23, 2010.

Peter McKnight   "What We Need Here Is a Bias in Favor of the Truth," *Vancouver Sun*, May 5, 2007.

Dean Miller   "Want Better Journalism? Boost News Literacy," *Christian Science Monitor*, January 14, 2010.

Kathleen Parker — "Viewpoints: Lessons from the Juan Williams Episode," *Atlanta Journal-Constitution*, October 27, 2010.

Richard Perez-Pen — "Online Watchdog Sniffs for Media Bias," *New York Times*, October 16, 2008.

Jeremy W. Peters — "Reuters Writer Resigns over Ethics Policy Breach," *New York Times*, October 19, 2010.

Pittsburgh Post-Gazette — "Ethics and Bias: Journalists Have More Than Their Share," February 7, 2005.

James Poniewozik — "Moderation in Excess," *Time*, November 16, 2009.

Cal Thomas — "American Journalism's Founding Fathers," *Times-Union*, March 3, 2006.

Ana Veciana-Suarez — "Everybody Discriminates in Some Way," *Miami Herald*, October 30, 2010.

Joan Vennochi — "Free Speech vs. Firing Offenses," *Boston Globe*, October 31, 2010.

John Wenzel — "'Democracy Now!' Host Wages War on War's Absence from National Dialogue," *Denver Post*, November 4, 2010.

Lane Williams   "Mormon Media Observer: Media
                     Bias More Complicated Than NPR
                     Decision Suggests," *Mormon Times*,
                     November 1, 2010.

Lane Witcover   "Analyst vs. Commentator: The
                     Difference. Juan Williams Firing
                     Episode Underscores Distinctions
                     Not Well Understood by the Public,"
                     Baltimore Sun, October 26, 2010.

Index